NEW SWAN SHAKESPEARE

GENERAL EDITOR

BERNARD LOTT, MA, Ph.D.

As You Like It

D0785774

As You Like It

Henry IV, Part I

Julius Caesar

Macbeth

The Merchant of Venice

A Midsummer Night's Dream

Much Ado About Nothing

Romeo and Juliet

The Tempest

Twelfth Night

WILLIAM SHAKESPEARE

As You Like It

EDITED BY
J W LEVER, M.A.

LONGMAN

Longman Group UK Limited,
Longman House, Burnt Mill, Harlow,
Essex CM20 2JE, England
and Associated Companies throughout the world.

This edition © Longman Group Ltd 1967

*First published * 1967*
Twenty-third impression 1990

ISBN 0-582-52725-2

Illustrations by H. C. McBeath

Produced by Longman Singapore Publishers Pte Ltd
Printed in Singapore

INTRODUCTION

The purpose of this book is to present Shakespeare's play in the simplest and most direct way. It is not a "simplified" text, nor does it attempt to provide all the information that a student may need. The text itself, which forms the greater part of the book, remains as the author wrote it (or as near to that ideal as we are now ever likely to come), though the spelling, punctuation and stage directions have been modernised. Everything added has only one aim: to help the reader in his understanding of this particular play. He may well need further help in widening his knowledge of Shakespeare, or of drama as an art. But his first need is to follow the play and what the characters are saying; it is this purpose which has been kept chiefly in mind throughout.

In order to make certain that the help given will in fact simplify the difficulties to be found in Shakespeare's work, and not just add more difficulties, explanations have been given within the range of a specially chosen list of 3,000 most commonly used English root-words. Every word in the book which falls outside this list is explained.

Words which are not used in modern English as Shakespeare used them, or which are not now used at all, will be found explained in notes on the pages facing the text. Because of changes in the use of the language, some phrases or sentences are explained as a whole in the notes; this is also done within the limits of the word-list.

Words which are still used in modern English, with their meaning unchanged, but which are not among the 3,000 root-words of the chosen list, will be found explained in the glossary at the back of the book, in the sense in which they appear.

A few words and expressions used in Shakespeare's time appear so frequently that there would be no point in explaining them in the notes on each occasion. Their meanings are given here:

an – "if".

ay (aye) – "yes".

become – often with the meaning of "suit" (as verb), e.g. *tears do not become a man*", III.iv.3.

coz – "cousin" (a shortened, affectionate form).

e'er – "ever".

ere – "before".

exeunt (Latin) – "they go out", i.e. leave the stage.

exit (Latin) – "he (she) goes out".

hence – "from this place".

hither – "to here".

methinks – "it seems to me (that)".

mine – "my" (sometimes – particularly when the word following begins with a vowel sound).

mistress, the lady with whom a man was in love; also used in politely addressing any lady.

nay – "no".

ne'er – "never".

o'er – "over".

prithee – "please" (short for "I pray thee").

quoth – "said".

sooth – "truth" (*in sooth*, "truthfully").

spake – "spoke".

ta'en – "taken; caught".

thou, thee (as object), *thy* (possessive), commonly used between friends where modern English uses *you*. See also *Verb forms* below this list.

whence – "from which place".

wherein – "in which place"; "in which way".

whither – "to which place".

withal, a strong form of *with* used at the end of a sentence.

ye – "you" (plural).

yea – "yes", "indeed".

yon, yond,

yonder – "that (one)"; "over there".

Verb forms: The verb associated with *thou* as subject ends in *-st* or *-est*, the common exceptions being *art* (are), *wert* (were), *wilt* (will), and *shalt* (shall), e.g. I.ii.6–10, *thou lovest . . . thou hadst* ("you had") *. . . So wouldst thou.*

The verb associated with *he, she* or a noun as subject sometimes ends in *-th* or *-eth*, e.g.

> . . . swears you do more usurp
> Than *doth* your brother that hath banished you (II.i.27).

The rest of the Introduction is arranged under the following headings:

vi

1 The Nature of the Play

As You Like It was probably written at some time between 1598 and 1600, and acted on the stage soon afterwards. Shakespeare was then about thirty-five years old; he had had a great deal of experience both as a dramatist and in the skilled work of producing plays for the theatre. He had written a number of comedies, including A Midsummer Night's Dream and The Merchant of Venice, nearly all his history plays connected with England, and the love-tragedy Romeo and Juliet. Although the greatest tragedies were still to be written, Shakespeare may be thought of as a dramatist who had already shown great power and variety in his work and whose ability to compose comedies was at its height. We may therefore expect to find in this play Shakespeare's usual mixture of humour, deep feeling and clear thought, with a highly developed understanding of human nature.

As You Like It is generally considered to be one of Shakespeare's most successful comedies. Most of its action is concerned with showing the adventures of lovers in a pleasant forest setting. At the end, all wrongs are put right and all the lovers are happily married. Darker and crueller elements, which are to be found in other comedies, such as the story of Shylock in The Merchant of Venice and of Don John in Much Ado About Nothing, do not affect events in this play after the first act. But this does not mean that suffering is altogether absent: if such were the case, the play would have nothing to do with real life. What we have rather is a story in which courage, sincerity and good sense win a victory over the evils in nature and society. Even in the love-affairs of the play, Shakespeare never forgets reality. In the Forest of Arden the characters learn that love is not just made up of fine ideals, noble thoughts and beautiful speeches, as most Elizabethan poets and romance-writers led their readers to suppose. Love must also be natural and express itself in terms of practical kindness and help. For most of us, love may, and usually does, include some folly. We are none the worse for it, provided that we learn to laugh, not only at others in love, but also at ourselves. For this reason the comedy is never cruel, just as the romance is never carried to extremes. Humour and sympathy are equally balanced.

2 The Story

The happenings in As You Like It were not taken from real life;

neither did Shakespeare invent them. The main story had already been told in a romance called *Rosalynde* by Thomas Lodge, printed in 1590. Rosalind, Celia (named Aliena), Orlando, and the two Dukes were among Lodge's characters. Shakespeare made the two Dukes brothers, added Touchstone and Audrey, shortened and changed most of the long speeches, and altered the ending. Lodge's romance, though written in prose, contained many poems supposed to have been made up by the characters; it was probably this that gave Shakespeare the idea of introducing poems by Orlando (III.ii) and Phebe's letter in verse (IV.iii), besides the songs, such as he usually put into his comedies. The Elizabethans enjoyed listening to poetry, and besides the verse in which some scenes were written, these poems and songs gave extra pleasure.

As a help to understanding the general design of *As You Like It*, a simple outline is provided here. At the beginning of each scene a more detailed account appears.

Events take place in an unnamed country, ruled by Duke Frederick, who has banished his brother the rightful Duke Senior. At Duke Frederick's court is his daughter Celia, and Rosalind, the daughter of the true Duke, who has been Celia's friend since their childhood. Meanwhile Duke Senior, with a few followers, lives in hiding in the Forest of Arden.

The play begins on the farm of Sir Rowland de Boys, a trusted friend of the true Duke. Sir Rowland has died, leaving his house and land to Oliver, the eldest of his three sons. Oliver's duty was to take care of his brothers Jaques and Orlando and provide for their education; but he lets Orlando grow up poor and ignorant. Orlando now demands his rights. In a fight with Oliver he shows that he is the stronger. Oliver, hating Orlando, encourages him to take part in a wrestling match at court with Charles, the Duke's best wrestler, and secretly plots for Charles to kill him. But instead Orlando wins. Rosalind, who has watched the wrestling, falls in love with Orlando, and Orlando finds he is equally in love with her.

Soon after, Duke Frederick banishes Rosalind from court, and she leaves to seek her father in the forest. Celia goes with her out of friendship, and Touchstone, the court "fool", keeps them company. For safety, Rosalind disguises herself as a boy, calling herself by the boy's name Ganymede, and pretending that Celia is her sister. Meanwhile

Orlando, on his way home, is met by Adam, his father's old servant, and advised to escape, as Oliver is again plotting against him. He leaves for Arden together with Adam.

In the forest the Duke and his followers pass their time cheerfully, except for Jaques, an old gentleman who has travelled a great deal and expresses sad, or mocking, reflections on life. Orlando meets Rosalind but does not recognise her in her disguise. Rosalind decides to test Orlando. She claims, as "Ganymede", to scorn love, and she says she will cure Orlando of his "disease". He is to come and woo her as if she were his Rosalind, and she will teach him how cruel and changeable girls can be. Orlando comes for a "lesson", and promises to return soon for another. However, he does not come. Oliver appears instead, and describes what has happened. Oliver too has now been banished. After wandering in the forest and falling asleep, he has been rescued by Orlando from a snake and a lioness that was about to kill him; but in the struggle Orlando has been wounded. Oliver is grateful to his brother for saving his life, and the old hatred has changed to love. When Rosalind hears this story, and sees a cloth stained with Orlando's blood, she faints. Oliver realises from this that she must be a girl in disguise.

This is not the only love-affair in Arden. Touchstone meets Audrey, a plain but sincere country girl, and decides to marry her. Silvius, a shepherd, woos the shepherdess Phebe, but she scorns him and falls in love with the disguised Rosalind, thinking her to be the boy Ganymede. Only at the end, when Phebe learns the truth, does she accept Silvius. Oliver loves Celia as soon as he sees her in the forest. All four pairs are at last happily married.

In the end it is reported that Duke Frederick, leading an army to attack Duke Senior and his followers, met a wise old man in the forest, who persuaded him to give up his rule and devote himself to a religious life. The true Duke goes back to rule his country, together with all his followers except Jaques, who chooses instead to join Duke Frederick in his new way of life. Orlando and Rosalind go with Duke Senior, Orlando as his heir.

It will be seen from this that the play combines two subjects. One is the story of the Duke and his brother, which brings out the great difference between true and false rulers. The relationship between Oliver and Orlando repeats the same idea in terms of family life, with one brother taking away the other brother's rights. The second subject is the love-affair of Orlando and Rosalind, together with the affairs of Silvius and Phebe, Touchstone and Audrey, Oliver and Celia. Here the difference is brought out between true and false love, while examples are provided of the way love can mean different things to different persons. Both subjects show a development from unnatural cruelty to natural kindness, from selfishness and hate to forgiveness and love. And in both stories the big change comes about through the experience of living in Arden.

3 The Characters

Duke Frederick is typical of the false ruler or tyrant. He governs the country through fear, banishing his opponents or threatening them with death. At the same time he has no control over his own feelings, but always fears that he will be betrayed, suspects those nearest to him, and breaks out into sudden violent anger. Although Orlando has shown himself brave at the wrestling match, he receives no praise or reward from Duke Frederick because his father was Frederick's enemy. Celia is made to feel ashamed of her own parent:

> My father's rough and envious disposition
> Sticks me at heart (1.ii.196).

In the next scene he enters "With his eyes full of anger" (1.iii.31) and suddenly banishes Rosalind. The only reasons for this are that she is Duke Senior's daughter, and that she is loved by the people for her own good qualities:

> Her very silence and her patience
> Speak to the people, and they pity her (1.iii.69).

Later, Duke Frederick suspects Orlando and sends Oliver to bring him back "dead or alive". Meanwhile he seizes all Oliver's land and property and drives him from his home. In the end he sets out for Arden, at the head of a great army, to capture the true Duke and kill him (v.iv); but fortunately for all, the "old religious man" he meets is able to turn him from his wickedness and change his whole nature.

Oliver is a similar character, though in private life he has less power than Frederick. His unkind treatment of his youngest brother is described in the first speech of the play. He calls Orlando "villain"

(I.i.44), which often had the meaning "low-born", although they are both sons of the same father, and he keeps from Orlando the small amount of money that has been left him by will. When Adam, the old true servant of the family, tries to make peace between them, Oliver insults him. Oliver is cunning as well as greedy, and lies to Charles about his brother (I.i.112-29) so that Charles will have reason to kill him. He later plans to burn down during the night the place where Orlando usually sleeps. Yet Oliver too is completely changed by Orlando's courage and kindness when in danger (IV.iii); and it is this changed man who falls in love with Celia and willingly gives up his father's estate to his brother.

Duke Senior and Orlando are exact opposites to their brothers. The true Duke has no fear of his followers, whom he addresses as "my co-mates and brothers in exile" (II.i.1). He is glad to be away from "the envious court", and welcomes the rough life of the forest. The winter's wind teaches him the truth about himself:

> This is no flattery; these are counsellors
> That feelingly persuade me what I am (II.i.10).

Speaking in "so quiet and so sweet a style", he shows full control over his feelings. When Orlando enters, threatening them all with a sword (II.vii), he answers him patiently, and gladly agrees to feed the young man and his old servant. Learning that Orlando is "the good Sir Rowland's son", he makes them both all the more welcome. At the end of the play he is glad to be united to Rosalind his daughter, and speaks as kindly to Celia, the daughter of his enemy. Gracious, good-hearted and wise, Duke Senior is, in contrast to Duke Frederick, a model ruler.

In Lodge's romance, *Orlando* had been a rather boastful, noisy character, and enjoyed fighting for its own sake. Shakespeare makes him more gentle and thoughtful, though not less brave. He boldly faces Charles the great wrestler, paying no attention to warnings that he is certain to lose, and refusing to let Rosalind and Celia stop the match. Yet after he has won, he is so nervous in the presence of the ladies that he forgets to thank them for their congratulations (I.ii.213-14). Orlando shows kindness towards his servant Adam, carrying him on his back in the forest when the old man is too weary to walk (II.vi) and refusing to eat until Adam has fed (II.vii.130-2).

Towards Rosalind, Orlando behaves like the typical lover of Elizabethan literature; he sighs for her and dreams of her, writing poems in her praise and hanging them on the trees of Arden. Jaques makes fun of him for all this, and so does Rosalind herself (III.ii). But Orlando is a man of action as well as a poet and lover. He wrestles with and defeats the famous Charles. He has every cause to hate Oliver; yet when Oliver is in danger he does not think of revenge, but risks his own life to save his brother's:

> But kindness, nobler ever than revenge,
> And nature, stronger than his just occasion,
> Made him give battle to the lioness (IV.iii.127).

Rosalind has indeed good reason for loving Orlando. He is not only handsome and a poet, but brave; not only brave but kind, thoughtful and forgiving.

Rosalind is the leading character of the play, and she more than any other gives to *As You Like It* its special quality. It is a mistake to think of her as quite simply a beautiful girl in love; but it is equally mistaken to regard her as no more than a sharp critic of other people's follies. She can sympathise with those who deserve sympathy, and also smile at her own weaknesses. When we see her first (I.ii), her thoughts are about her banished father, and she only talks of love to entertain Celia; but soon she is full of admiration for Orlando, and love makes her sad and silent (I.iii). In Arden, however, and disguised as a boy, she has a chance to speak freely to all kinds of people, including Orlando, and to apply her clear, clever mind to their problems. By these means Rosalind, though deeply in love herself, is able to criticise and help others. She is, of course, pleased that Orlando writes verses to her; but in the character of Ganymede she makes fun of him for going to such foolish extremes:

> There is a man haunts the forest, that abuses our young plants with carving "Rosalind" on their barks . . . deifying the name of Rosalind. If I could meet that fancy-monger, I would give him some good counsel (III.ii.311).

She promises to cure him of love by showing him the true nature of women – "changeable, longing and liking, proud, fantastical, apish, shallow, inconstant" (III.ii.352) – and, as Ganymede pretending to be Rosalind, behaves much in this way towards him. She warns Orlando that women change after they are married: they are "May when they are maids, but the sky changes when they are wives" (IV.i.122). She tells him that, in spite of all that the poets have said, no man ever died for love (IV.i.77–88). Yet all this is only to test the sincerity of Orlando's passion, and in the same scene Rosalind admits to Celia that she herself is "many fathom deep" in love. The reality of this love appears most plainly when she learns that Orlando has been wounded. Then she is unable to keep up her pretence of being a boy, and faints from shock (IV.iii).

It is just because Rosalind is, in spite of her disguise, a woman, that she criticises Phebe so severely. Rosalind reminds the scornful, spoilt shepherdess that she will not always be young and beautiful, and tells her plainly that Silvius is a better man than she is woman. Her advice is,

> . . . know yourself; down on your knees,
> And thank heaven, fasting, for a good man's love (III.v.107).

But Rosalind's clear understanding does not lead her to despair of human beings, or to put on an appearance of sadness so as to seem wise. She has a low opinion, therefore, of Jaques, who wishes to be thought a philosopher because of his travels and experiences:

> I had rather have a fool to make me merry than experience to make me sad – and to travel for it too . . . Farewell, Monsieur Traveller (IV.i.22, 27).

As a critic of Orlando, of Silvius and Phebe, and of Jaques, Rosalind presents the realistic view of life which balances romantic extremes in Shakespeare's comedies. Yet since she is in love herself, and we are in sympathy with her feelings, this realism is balanced in turn by our understanding that love, so long as it goes with kindness and good sense, is necessary for human happiness.

Celia is a fit companion for Rosalind; she is clever and amusing, and at the same time sincere and to be trusted. Because she has no reason to like her father, and through most of the play is not in love with anyone, she makes less appeal to our sympathy; but in deciding to leave Duke Frederick's court and go with Rosalind into Arden she proves that she is a true friend. Rosalind has confidence in her and reveals to her all her secret thoughts. Celia often makes fun of Rosalind's admiration for Orlando. She keeps Rosalind waiting a long time before telling her that the author of the verses she reads to Rosalind is Orlando (III.ii), and her description of him makes him look foolish:

I found him under a tree, like a dropped acorn (III.ii.206).

She plays with Rosalind's feelings about Orlando, suggesting that he is not as true as he claims to be:

Celia   Nay, certainly, there is no truth in him.

Rosalind Do you think so?

Celia   Yes . . .

Rosalind Not true in love?

Celia   Yes, when he is in, but I think he is not in.

$$(III.iv.17)$$

But all this is intended to warn Rosalind against taking love too earnestly and suffering disappointment. Celia acts as the witness in IV.i to the promise of marriage that Orlando and Rosalind make to one another. In Elizabethan times a promise of this kind in front of a witness was considered a full marriage in law (though marriage in church was also required); it is therefore important to the story that Celia is present here. Although Celia seems so cool-headed and controlled, she too falls in love as soon as she meets Oliver (IV.iii). Like every other young person in the play, she finds that reason without serious feeling is not enough.

Touchstone, the "fool" of Duke Frederick, is by no means foolish in his judgments. His name means a stone used for testing the value of metals, and he is in fact a critic of what is truly valuable in men and society. Jaques describes him well:

> in his brain,
> . . . he hath strange places crammed
> With observation, the which he vents
> In mangled forms (II.vii.38, 40).

He has, that is, a strange, twisted way of making wise remarks so that they sound amusing. An example of this is his story of the knight and the pancakes (I.ii.52-65), the point of which is that some fools have more honour than noblemen. Again, in his argument with the shepherd Corin (III.ii), he seems to suggest that people at court are better than those in the country, but really shows that, if anything, they are worse. He seems to be mocking himself when he describes his love for Jane Smile (II.iv.40-8); actually he is showing the folly of "all nature in love", including Rosalind. His imitation of Orlando's poem,

> If a hart do lack a hind,
> Let him seek out Rosalind.
> If the cat will after kind,
> So be sure will Rosalind (III.ii.87).

brings out the fact that the love of Orlando and Rosalind, in spite of all their romantic beliefs, is basically the same as any other human attraction.

Touchstone, though he pretends to be simple, is quite well educated. He has heard of the Roman poet Ovid, who had to live among the Goths, and through clever word-play compares this with his own life in the country, among the goats (III.iii.5-6). He talks nonsense to William, Audrey's lover, because William would not know the difference between this and deep learning; but his very way of expressing himself shows that he is acquainted with philosophical ideas and "figures in rhetoric" (v.i.35). Above all, he is a practical man. He may have no use for romantic love or poetry, but he finds himself a wife in Arden because, like every other man in Shakespeare's view, he too needs marriage. We may not think that Touchstone's view of life is sufficient, but it provides a useful check against the opposite extreme of too much idealism.

Our opinion of "the melancholy Jaques" changes as the play goes on. He seems at first to be a thoughtful man, with a philosophical mind that seeks to "moralise" or draw a moral, from all that he sees. The stag wounded in the forest and deserted by his companions (II.i) reminds Jaques of the way men behave towards the poor and unfortunate. He points out all the evils in the court, city, and country, and shows that even Duke Senior and his followers treat the animals like tyrants. He realises, as has been seen, that Touchstone is a "wise fool", who also likes to "moralise". All this is interesting, and his speech, "All the world's a stage", is one of the best known in Shakespeare's plays (although the same basic idea had been expressed by many other writers). But gradually we come to feel that Jaques enjoys his own weary sadness too much; that it is all a way of appearing wiser than others; and that his view of life would leave out all that is good and helpful. When Jaques remarks, "I can suck melancholy . . . as a weasel sucks eggs" (II.v.11), we remember that the weasel is a destructive animal. The Duke points out that Jaques has himself led a wild and pleasure-loving life, and now blames others for the same faults (II.vii.64-9). Orlando refuses to join him in speaking bitterly against "our mistress the world", saying modestly:

I will chide no breather in the world but myself, against whom I know most faults (III.ii.246).

Nor will he allow Jaques to describe love as his "worst fault":

'T is a fault I will not change for your best virtue. I am weary of you (III.ii.249).

Rosalind has the same poor opinion of Jaques; she dislikes his affected manner of speech and dress, and his way of running down his own country in order that everyone should know he has travelled abroad.

It is clear that by the end of the play we are meant to distrust Jaques's ideas. They seem more limited even than the coarse common sense of Touchstone, less likely to make anyone happy than the generous idealism of Orlando and Rosalind. To understand how Shakespeare came to invent the character of Jaques, it should be realised that Jaques's way of seeing life had become fashionable at this time, and that many courtiers of Queen Elizabeth liked to draw attention to themselves by dressing and speaking like "melancholy men". This was Shakespeare's answer to such pretences. On the other hand, much that Jaques had to say was true, even if it was not the whole truth. Nor does Jaques harm anyone. He prevents Touchstone and Audrey from going through an illegal form of marriage as conducted by Sir Oliver Mar-text, the ignorant unqualified priest (III.iii). And if in the end he refuses to go back to court with Duke Senior and the rest, it is not because he is disloyal, but because he hopes to learn a truer wisdom from the "old religious man" who has changed the life of Duke Frederick. What Jaques needs, in fact, is to become more sincere and more fully conscious of his own past faults.

Of the other characters in Arden, little need be said. *Corin, Silvius, Phebe, William* and *Audrey* form a group of simple country people. *Corin* has a wisdom that comes not from education but from a lifetime of honest work. As Touchstone says, "Such a one is a natural philosopher" (III.ii.27). In a few words, Corin sums up the kind of man he is:

> Sir, I am a true labourer: I earn that I eat, get that I wear, owe no man hate, envy no man's happiness, glad of other men's good, content with my harm, and the greatest of my pride is to see my ewes graze and my lambs suck (III.ii.62).

Silvius and *Phebe* are more like the country people imagined by Elizabethan poets than real shepherds and shepherdesses. Songs, poems and plays about scornful shepherd girls and devoted young shepherds were much in fashion. The subject was considered to be pretty and poetic, and appealed especially to people living in towns. Shakespeare thought otherwise. He put these characters into his play in such a way that the proud Phebe made a fool of herself by wooing Rosalind, and Silvius by carrying a love-letter to another "man". Rosalind has some stern advice to give to both of them before they marry. *William* and *Audrey* are far more like real shepherds; but William is so simple that nobody regrets it when Touchstone makes fun of him (v.i). He himself hardly seems to mind when Audrey gives him up. Audrey, however, has some true merit. She is plain, awkward and ignorant; but she is also honest and virtuous. When Touchstone says he wishes she were "poetical", her answer is:

> I do not know what "poetical" is. Is it honest in deed and word? Is it a true thing? (III.iii.13)

These are the qualities of character Audrey desires. And Touchstone himself recognises her virtues when he says of her:

> Rich honesty dwells like a miser, sir, in a poor house, as your pearl in your foul oyster (v.iv.56).

It was common in Shakespeare's time for writers either to describe country people as foolish and laughable, or else to make them all into lovers and philosophers, more passionate or wiser than anyone else.

Shakespeare shows them as they really were, sometimes stupid, sometimes sensible as a result of experience, and usually honest and straightforward. Silvius and Phebe are exceptions, but by including them Shakespeare only underlined the difference between the romantic way of treating such characters and the realistic. The general picture is true, and part of the true experience that the Forest of Arden provides for everyone in the play.

4 Construction and Ideas

There are, we have noticed, two main subjects in *As You Like It*: tyranny and true authority; and love, true and false. When the play begins, the tyrant, Duke Frederick, is in power and his brother, the true Duke Senior, is poor and in hiding. The subject is given more force by a further example from private life, where Oliver enjoys his father's wealth while his youngest brother Orlando is neglected and badly treated. At the end of the play Duke Senior returns to power with his loyal followers, and Orlando, married to Rosalind, becomes his heir. Frederick changes places with his brother, to pass his life in religious study, and Oliver, married to Celia, finds happiness in a peaceful country life. In this comedy, then, no one takes revenge and no one is punished. The virtuous receive their reward, the wicked regret their evil and change their character. As for the love-story, Orlando and Rosalind are true to each other; but Orlando has to be cured of too poetic and idealistic a way of regarding his lady, and Rosalind's love becomes a truly deep affection when she hears that Orlando has been wounded. Silvius spoils his shepherdess by being too humble, and she behaves vainly and selfishly. Phebe is fit for marriage only when she finds that she has neglected a faithful lover and "thrown herself" at Rosalind, who is not even a man. Touchstone at first scorns Audrey, and plans an illegal marriage that will give him an excuse to get rid of her later. But when he does come to marry Audrey he has found out her virtues, and the marriage may well last, in spite of Jaques's mockery. As for Oliver and Celia, their love at first sight would not be very convincing were it not that Oliver is now a changed man. He has become kind and grateful, and is likely to respect Celia's own good qualities.

Some critics believe that the happy ending of this play is artificial. It seems to them that the wicked change their natures too easily, and that everything works out better than it possibly could in life. There is some truth in the criticism. Certainly Shakespeare brings the change about very suddenly. Oliver speaks of his own feelings only in a few lines.

> 'T was I, but 't is not I: I do not shame
> To tell you what I was, since my conversion
> So sweetly tastes, being the thing I am (IV.iii.134).

And we hear of Duke Frederick's decision only through Jaques de Boys' report (V.iv.139–54). It would have been better, perhaps, if more space had been given to these changes of heart. But Shakespeare knew that audiences expected comedies to end happily, just as they expected tragedies to end sadly, and he often did not take much trouble with the exact details of how evil in a character turns to good.

However, the idea of a change of heart is suggested in the play by other means. The first indication is in I.ii, where Rosalind and Celia argue jokingly about Nature and Fortune. Which is more important? Fortune – the kind of luck which makes men great and happy, or poor and wretched, without deserving it? Or Nature – which causes love between brothers, or friends, or man and woman? The answer of *As You Like It* is Nature, which wins in the end. And Shakespeare's way of presenting Nature is through the Forest of Arden. After the first act, practically the whole play is set in Arden. Although there are not many exciting events there, all the experiences of the characters take place in the forest. Indeed, Arden is an experience in itself.

Elizabethan authors were fond of describing some beautiful natural setting where simple shepherds lived. Nobody worked very hard there; there was enough plain food, the sun always shone; most of the time was spent in making love, composing songs, and talking wisely about life and virtue. No such place, of course, ever existed, though ancient poets believed it did long ago in the "Golden Age". *Pastoral* poems and romances (i.e. about the life of shepherds in this ideal setting) provided a kind of dream world for readers at courts and in big cities, who thought they might be happy if they could live the simple life in this way. Shakespeare took the idea of the Forest of Arden from Lodge's romance, which was of the same "pastoral" type, but he made it into something very different. It is a serious mistake to think of Arden as just an escape from the difficulties of life.

This is not a place of eternal summer; Duke Senior speaks of

> the icy fang
> And churlish chiding of the winter's wind (II.i.6).

and the song, "Blow, blow, thou winter wind" (II.vii.173) brings this lesson home to us. There is hunger in the forest: Orlando and Adam nearly starve to death. There are wild beasts there – the snake and the lioness that threaten Oliver. The shepherds do not live comfortably: Corin complains of a selfish master who is selling the cottage Corin lives in (II.iv.74-6). Even among the animals there is cruelty of one to another, as is made clear in the story of the wounded stag (II.i.29-57). No wonder that Touchstone, as a realist, cannot say for sure which is better, the court or the country.

Arden is to be understood not as an escape from life, but as a way to find its truth. There one faces realities without the deceit and falsehood of life at court. And so Duke Senior welcomes the winter without shelter, since

> This is no flattery; these are counsellors
> That feelingly persuade me what I am (II.i.10).

The winter wind in Amiens' song is "not so unkind as man's ingratitude". If "most friendship is feigning, most loving mere folly", in Arden one discovers the difference between true friendship and false, between wise and foolish love. As Dr Helen Gardner writes:*

> Arden is a place of discovery where the truth becomes clear and where each man finds himself and his true way.

In Arden, not only wild nature, but human nature too, works freely. It is here, where Orlando saves his life, that Oliver finds natural love between brothers to be more important than greed for possessions. Here, as they face hardship together, Celia and Rosalind prove that their friendship is real. Here Duke Frederick meets the "old religious man" who, living alone, has had time to think of the true values in life, and he decides that it matters more to learn about these than to rule a country over which he has no right. And here the various pairs of lovers come to an understanding of love.

Most of the play is taken up with these love stories, in which romance and comedy are mixed. In considering the characters, it

---

*More Talking of Shakespeare, ed. John Garrett, Longmans 1959.

becomes clear that each had a part to play in criticising the mistakes and follies of the other. The chief critic is Rosalind, who is greatly helped by her boy's disguise, as this enables her to speak more freely. Had she made fun of Orlando's love in her own person, instead of as the boy Ganymede, she might well have driven him away. Her advice to Phebe is more forceful because she speaks like a proud, scornful youth; and Phebe comes to understand her folly only through falling in love with a girl in disguise. But this is not all. Rosalind, too, in her real character is made fun of by both Touchstone and Celia. Touchstone is mocked by Jaques, who is mocked in turn by both Orlando and Rosalind. Like the winds in the forest, clear, sharp criticism blows through all the characters. If Silvius is to blame for making his shepherdess into a poetic fancy, Touchstone is too coarse in thinking of Audrey as just the answer to a passing need. Orlando and Rosalind find a balance between romance and realism, between fancy and nature; but only as a result of seeing the follies of others and having their own follies pointed out to them. Even experience can be harmful if made into a master of one's life instead of a means to happiness. Jaques seems wise, but his pride in seeming sadder and wiser than others is itself foolish.

5 The Style

As usual in Shakespeare's comedies, there is great variety in ways of expression. This is necessary in order to suggest differences of character and ways of regarding life. People of high rank, such as Duke Frederick or Duke Senior, usually speak in "blank verse", a kind of verse without rhyme but having five clear beats in each line. For example:

> Hére feel we nót the pénaltý of Adam,
> The séasons' dífference; ás the ícy fáng
> And chúrlish chíding óf the wínter's wínd,
> Whích, when it bítes and blóws upón my bódy
> Éven till I shrínk with cóld, I smíle and sáy
> "Thís is no fláttery . . ." (ii.i.5)

But since the effect is thoughtful and dignified, the style may be used by any character on a serious occasion. In i.i, where Orlando and Adam are carrying on a normal conversation, they speak prose; but when in II.iii they must make important decisions, they speak in blank verse. Similarly Rosalind and Celia usually speak to one another in prose, as is suitable for the light conversation of two close friends; but when, in I.iii, Duke Frederick banishes Rosalind, and Celia chooses to go with her, there is a change to blank verse. When Jaques expresses his considered thoughts, as in II.vii.138ff., he speaks in blank verse; in conversation with Orlando, however, he uses prose (III.ii.223ff.). Often the changes are made very delicately, almost in the way a composer of music chooses which instrument he wishes to use. To suggest the purely emotional expression of love, a kind of verse with short lines and frequent rhymes is made use of, as in the poetry Orlando writes to Rosalind:

> Fróm the eást to wéstern Índ,
> No jéwel ís like Rósalínd (III.ii.74).

Phebe's poem to "Ganymede" is of the same sort:

> Árt thou gód, to shépherd túrned,
> Thát a máiden's héart hath búrned? (IV.iii.40)

Touchstone in contrast, with his hard common sense, speaks only prose, except where he makes up verses in mockery of Orlando's (III.ii.87–98). For a variety of effect, Shakespeare at times introduces songs. Besides providing a change from ordinary speech, they also help to suggest the "feeling" of the play at that point. "Under the greenwood tree" (II.v) is full of cheerfulness in the face of "winter and rough weather"; "Blow, blow, thou winter wind" (II.vii), a much sadder song, comes from the arrival of poor old Adam carried in by Orlando. "It was a lover and his lass" (v.iii) is well suited to the happier emotions towards the end of the play, and the last song, "Wedding is great Juno's crown" has the more stately quality that fits a celebration of marriage.

Much of *As You Like It* is written in a kind of prose which is full of word-play, unusual images and comparisons, which need careful attention if we are to understand the meaning properly. This is especially true of the conversations of Rosalind and Celia, and the talk of Touchstone. Shakespeare's aim was not, of course, to make his play hard to follow. He wanted his audience and his readers to enjoy the quick, clever thought, the sudden and unexpected turns of ideas, and to like his characters for their minds as well as their emotions.

6 Imagery

All education in Shakespeare's time was based on a study of "the classics", chiefly the literature of ancient Rome. Just as today English poems and plays are read by people with a different language and often different religious beliefs, so Elizabethan readers formed their knowledge of literature from Latin, with its references to Greek and Roman heroes, gods and goddesses. For this reason we find in *As You Like It* frequent mention of Venus and Cupid, Jove and Juno. Orlando compares Rosalind with Helen, Cleopatra and other famous figures of classical literature and history (III.ii.130ff.). Rosalind refers to Troilus and Leander when telling Orlando that no man really died for love (IV.i.79ff.). Jaques compares the knowledge of Touchstone, seemingly a fool, with Jove in a thatched house (III.iii.7–8). And when the couples are to be married in the play's last scene, Hymen, the Roman god of marriage, conducts the ceremony. In spite of this, all the characters are to be regarded as living in Shakespeare's own time, as having Christian beliefs, and as being married according to the proper religious practice of the sixteenth century. The Roman and non-Christian references should be seen as part of the poetic colouring of the play; especially to be expected because *As You Like It* used a pastoral story as in classical literature, with the old names Silvius, Phebe and Corin for the pastoral characters of Arden.

Apart from this, the commonest imagery in the play brought to mind hunting or some other sport. Orlando sees himself as a "quintain" (I.ii.207); Touchstone describes lovers as running into "strange capers" (II.iv.47); Jaques thinks that for innocent persons his mockery "like a wild goose flies" (II.vii.86); Orlando compares Rosalind with a "huntress" (III.ii.4); Duke Senior says that Touchstone "uses his folly like a stalking-horse" (v.iv.94). The effect is to suggest an active, outdoor life such as suits the setting of Arden. Even closer to the central idea of the play are the images of cleaning and purifying. Jaques offers to "Cleanse the foul body of the infected world" (II.vii.60); Rosalind promises Orlando "to wash your liver as clean as a sound sheep's heart" (III.ii.361); Touchstone asks doubters to "put me to my purgation" (v.iv.42). Such imagery helps to suggest the purifying though stern action of the forest upon those living in it.

It has been mentioned that the conversation of Rosalind and Celia about Fortune and Nature in I.ii draws attention to one of the chief ideas of the play. The contrast between fortune and nature is brought out by frequent references: Celia wishes to "mock the good house-wife Fortune from her wheel" (I.ii.26); Amiens speaks of Duke Senior's power to "translate the stubbornness of fortune" (II.i.19); Adam refers to fortune's recompense in death (II.iii.75–6); Corin wishes his "fortunes" were more able to relieve Celia (II.iv.71); Jaques mentions that Touchstone "railed on Lady Fortune in good terms" (II.vii.16); and so on. While Fortune is cruel or false to man, Nature, though often stern, is honest and true. Simple Corin is described as "a natural philosopher" (III.ii.27); the proud Phebe is "the ordinary Of nature's sale-work" (III.v.42); and it is nature, "stronger than his just occasion" (for revenge), that made Orlando fight the lioness to save Oliver (IV.iii.128).

Some of the devices used by Shakespeare to strengthen the effect of language and to present exciting images to the minds of his audiences are worth naming. In several of the examples used above in connection with the contrast between fortune and nature, these two ideas are *personified*, that is, spoken about as if they are persons rather than ideas.

> Though Nature hath given us wit to flout at Fortune, hath not
> Fortune sent in this fool to cut off the argument? (I.ii.38)

We apply the name *simile* to a direct comparison between the subject treated and the image which that subject suggests, but the comparison (often introduced by *like*, or *as*) is to one quality only. When Duke Senior offers us the simile of the toad,

> Sweet are the uses of adversity,
> Which, like the toad, ugly and venomous,
> Wears yet a precious jewel in his head (II.i.12)

we are not expected to compare adversity (hardship) to a toad in every way – only to the idea of the value that there can be in something otherwise so unpleasant.

A *metaphor* is a comparison which is only suggested, not made directly. Words used metaphorically refer at once to two or more different things brought to the mind together. We see both the world with its children growing up, its grown-ups growing older, and the theatre stage with its busy actors in the famous lines:

> All the world 's a stage,
> And all the men and women merely players:
> They have their exits and their entrances,
> And one man in his time plays many parts (II.vii.138).

Jaques does not say that the world is like a stage and that men are like actors, but that the world *is* a stage; the listener decides for himself in what ways this is true.

There is frequent use of *irony* in *As You Like It*. When Touchstone has been told, in answer to his question, that the sport that the ladies would have enjoyed is a series of wrestling matches in which ribs have been broken and men killed, his remark

> Thus men may grow wiser every day (I.ii.109).

is irony: his words express the opposite of his real meaning – Le Beau has offered him a piece of nonsense, not of wisdom. In a comedy which includes disguise there is every opportunity for *dramatic irony*, where an actor's words mean one thing to the person he is speaking to and another thing to the audience. When Rosalind says to Phebe:

> I pray you, do not fall in love with me,
> For I am falser than vows made in wine (III.v.71).

Phebe hears the young man, Ganymede, claiming that he is a deceiver, but the audience knows how "false" Ganymede really is – not a man at all, but a girl in disguise.

7 As You Like It *as a comedy*

Some people think of a comedy as a number of amusing situations, full of enjoyable nonsense, in which one laughs at all the difficulties the characters get mixed up in. This is more correctly called "farce". Another idea of comedy is a serious play which shows up various kinds of human folly and teaches good sense. Ben Jonson, Shakespeare's friend, wrote plays of this sort. Besides this, comedy can be mainly a play about adventure and love. Shakespeare's comedies, however, combine all these qualities. Love-making and romance, political ideas, views on proper human conduct, are brought together in such a way that there is poetry and laughter, nonsense and sense. *As You Like It* opens with a story of tyranny and injustice, and there is a certain touch of sadness even in the happier scenes in Arden. But soon the gay, clever conversation of Rosalind and Celia breaks in on this, suggesting a more hopeful way out for people with high spirits and clear minds. Love is the main subject for much of the play, but reason and the power to laugh at foolish extremes keep romance in check. The mistakes brought out by disguise add some farce to the effect and this will be more amusing if we remember that in Shakespeare's time the women's parts were acted by boys. Rosalind disguised as Ganymede is therefore a boy acting the part of a girl acting the part of a boy! Most important of all is the working of nature in Arden, which in the end prevails over fortune and its cruelty. Nature brings brothers together, binds friendship, and unites lovers. It allows for some foolishness in love and some common-sense criticism, but is opposed to too much reason and too much folly. We can laugh, therefore, at Orlando and Rosalind, yet at the same time sympathise with them, since they appeal to our good nature. In this broad-minded, generous comedy it is right that several pairs of lovers, each different in their way of loving, should find a common road to happiness in marriage. As Jaques remarks, "There is, sure, another flood toward, and these couples are coming to the ark" (v.iv.35). The "flood" is old age and death, which sweeps away every generation; and the "ark" into which we enter, two by two, is marriage, which results in new life. Such is the way of nature, to be learned in Arden, which holds society together, provides for love and happiness, and makes sure that the human race will continue. For Shakespeare, this is the main subject of comedy, and in no play perhaps so clearly as in *As You Like It*.

SHORT READING LIST FOR MORE SENIOR STUDENTS

For details of Shakespearian word-meaning, students may consult:

A Shakespeare Glossary, by C. T. Onions, Oxford University Press, 1911, repr. 1958.

Explorations in Shakespeare's Language, by Hilda M. Hulme, Longmans, 1962.

Shakespeare-Lexicon, by A. Schmidt, de Gruyter, Berlin, 1923.

For Shakespeare's ideas, imagery and word-play:

Shakespeare and the Nature of Man, by Theodore Spencer, Macmillan, 1942.

The Development of Shakespeare's Imagery, by W. H. Clemen, Methuen, 1951.

Shakespeare and Elizabethan Poetry, by M. C. Bradbrook, Cambridge University Press, 1951.

Shakespeare's World of Images, by D. A. Stauffer, Oxford University Press, 1952.

Shakespeare's Word-Play, by M. M. Mahood, Methuen, 1957.

For Shakespeare, his theatre and his times:

A Companion to Shakespeare Studies, ed. H. Granville Barker and G. B. Harrison, Cambridge University Press, 1934.

Shakespeare's Theatre, by C. Walter Hodges, Oxford University Press, 1964.

For a selection of Shakespearian criticism:

Shakespeare and his Critics, by F. E. Halliday, Duckworth, 1958.

For a study of the sources of the play:

Shakespeare's Sources, by Kenneth Muir, Volume I, Methuen, 1957.

Narrative and Dramatic Sources of Shakespeare, by G. Bullough, Volume II, Routledge & Kegan Paul, 1958.

For a study of *As You Like It* and Shakespearian Comedy:

Shakespeare and the Romance Tradition, by E. C. Pettet, Staples Press, 1949.

Shakespeare and his Comedies, by John Russell Brown, Methuen, 1957 (second edition, 1962).

Shakespeare's Comedies, by Bertrand Evans, Oxford University Press, 1960.

Shakespeare's Happy Comedies, by John Dover Wilson, Faber, 1962.

Shakespeare Survey 8, article by Harold Jenkins, "As You Like It", Cambridge University Press, 1955.

More Talking of Shakespeare, ed. John Garrett, articles by Helen Gardner, "As You Like It", and Mary Lascelles, "Shakespeare's Pastoral Comedy", Longmans, 1959.

DRAMATIS PERSONAE

DUKE SENIOR, *in banishment in the Forest of Arden*
DUKE FREDERICK, *his brother, usurper of the Dukedom*
AMIENS ⎫
JAQUES ⎭ *lords attending on Duke Senior*
LE BEAU, *a courtier*
CHARLES, *a wrestler*
OLIVER ⎫
JAQUES ⎬ *sons of Sir Rowland de Boys*
ORLANDO ⎭
ADAM ⎫
DENNIS ⎭ *servants of Oliver*
TOUCHSTONE, *a clown*
SIR OLIVER MAR-TEXT, *a vicar*
CORIN ⎫
SILVIUS ⎭ *shepherds*
WILLIAM, *a country fellow*
HYMEN

ROSALIND, *daughter of Duke Senior*
CELIA, *daughter of Duke Frederick*
PHEBE, *a shepherdess*
AUDREY, *a country girl*

LORDS, PAGES, FORESTERS, AND ATTENDANTS

The scenes are laid at Oliver's house; the Duke's court; and in the Forest of Arden.

(1.i) Orlando complains to the old servant Adam about the bad treatment he has received from Oliver, his eldest brother, since their father's death. Oliver arrives and speaks to Orlando scornfully; they fight, and Orlando shows himself the stronger. In revenge, Oliver plots with Charles, Duke Frederick's wrestler, arranging for Charles to kill Orlando at the match to be held next day in front of the Duke. Mention is made of how the true Duke, Duke Senior, Frederick's brother, lives with a few of his supporters in hiding in the Forest of Arden.

1 *it was upon . . . crowns* – "in this way there was left *(bequeathed)* to me by (my father's) will only the small amount of 1,000 *crowns* (gold coins worth 25p each)". (Orlando and Adam enter in the middle of a conversation.)

2 *charged . . . blessing* – "my brother was ordered *(charged)*, as a condition for his (our father's) blessing".

3 *breed me* – "bring me up, educate me".

4 *report . . . profit* – "the reports speak most favourably *(goldenly)* of how he is benefiting from it *(his profit)*".

5 *rustically* – "like a farm labourer".

6 *stays . . . unkept* – "keeps me back here at home unprovided for *(unkept)*". There is word-play on *keeps*, line 5, and *unkept*.

7 *call . . . keeping* – "do you call it proper provision".

8 *differs . . . ox* – "is not different from the way an ox is fed in its stall".

9 *besides . . . fair* – "in addition to being healthy".

10 *manage* – "correct way of moving", i.e. the horses may be said to have an education; Orlando has none.

11 *to that end . . . hired* – "for that purpose, riders are hired at a high price".

12 *but growth* – "except the mere fact that I grow".

13 *bound* – "owing a duty".

14 *Besides . . . take from me* (line 15) – "As well as so generously *(plentifully)* giving me nothing in this way, he seems by his special favour *(countenance)* to take away the one special quality *(the something)* that I was given by nature". (Nature had given Orlando one good quality: he was born a gentleman. Oliver was trying to take away that quality.) Orlando's use of *plentifully* and *countenance* when he really means the opposite is an example of irony (see Introduction, p. xxv).

15 *hinds* – "farm servants".

16 *bars me* – "keeps me from".

17 *as much as . . . education* – "as far as he has the power, is gradually destroying the good qualities of my birth *(gentility)* through my (lack of) up-bringing and training *(mines* – "undermines, tries to destroy from below")".

18 *Go apart* – "Move a short distance away".

19 *shake me up* – "scold me roughly".

ACT ONE

Scene I. The orchard of Oliver's house.
Enter ORLANDO *and* ADAM.

ORLANDO

As I remember, Adam, it was upon this fashion[1] bequeathed me by will but poor a thousand crowns, and, as thou sayest, charged my brother on his blessing[2] to breed me[3] well; and there begins my sadness. My brother Jaques he keeps at school, and report[4] speaks goldenly of his profit. For my part, he keeps me rustically[5] at home or, to speak more properly, stays[6] me here at home unkept; for call you that keeping[7] for a gentleman of my birth, that differs[8] not from the stalling of an ox? His horses are bred better; for besides that they are fair[9] with their feeding, they are taught their manage,[10] and to that end[11] riders dearly hired, but I, his brother, gain nothing under him but growth,[12] for the which his animals on his dunghills are as much bound[13] to him as I. Besides this nothing[14] that he so plentifully gives me, the something that nature gave me, his countenance seems to take from me. He lets me feed with his hinds,[15] bars me[16] the place of a brother, and, as much as in him lies,[17] mines my gentility with my education. This is it, Adam, that grieves me; and the spirit of my father, which I think is within me, begins to mutiny against this servitude. I will no longer endure it, though yet I know no wise remedy how to avoid it.

Enter OLIVER

ADAM

Yonder comes my master, your brother.

ORLANDO

Go apart,[18] Adam, and thou shalt hear how he will shake me up.[19]
[ADAM *stands back*

1

20 *Now . . . make you* – "Well, what are you doing" (in reply, Orlando uses *make* in its more usual sense; *sir* is unfriendly rather than respectful).

21 *Marry* – "Indeed".

22 *be naught awhile* – "do not trouble me for a time".

23 *What prodigal . . . wasted* – "What share of wealth have I wasted" (a reference to the Bible story – Luke 15:11–32 – of the *prodigal* (wasteful) son who spent his entire share of his father's wealth and had to eat with the hogs).

24 *Know . . . are*, i.e. "Do you know that you are standing in front of your master". (Orlando pretends not to understand him.)

25 *him I am before* – "the man I am standing in front of", i.e. Oliver.

26 *in the gentle . . . blood* – "because I am of the same noble *(gentle)* blood".

27 *The courtesy . . . first-born* – "The custom of civilised nations grants *(allows)* that, as the son who was born first, you are in authority over me *(my better)*".

28 *takes not . . . betwixt us* – "makes me still a man of noble birth, and would do that even if there were *(were there)* twenty brothers between us", i.e. even if Orlando were the twenty-second son, he would still be noble by birth.

29 *albeit . . . reverence* – "although, I admit, the fact that you were born before me does make you older".

OLIVER

Now, sir, what make[20] you here?

ORLANDO

Nothing; I am not taught to make anything.   25

OLIVER

What mar you then, sir?

ORLANDO

Marry,[21] sir, I am helping you to mar that which God made, a
poor unworthy brother of yours, with idleness.

OLIVER

Marry, sir, be better employed, and be naught awhile.[22]

ORLANDO

Shall I keep your hogs, and eat husks with them? What prodigal[23]   30
portion have I spent that I should come to such penury?

OLIVER

Know you[24] where you are, sir?

ORLANDO

O, sir, very well: here in your orchard.

OLIVER

Know you before whom, sir?

ORLANDO

Ay, better than him I am before[25] knows me. I know you are my   35
eldest brother, and in the gentle condition of blood,[26] you should
so know me. The courtesy[27] of nations allows you my better in
that you are the first-born, but the same tradition takes not[28]
away my blood, were there twenty brothers betwixt us. I have
as much of my father in me as you, albeit,[29] I confess, your   40
coming before me is nearer to his reverence.

3

30 *you are . . . in this* – "you have too little experience of fighting" (Orlando shows his meaning by grasping Oliver's throat and making him powerless to move).

31 *I am no . . . begot villains* – "I am not a man of low birth (*villain*); I am Sir Rowland de Boys' youngest son, and anyone who says that the sons of such a father are men of low birth *(villains)* is himself a wicked man *(villain)* three times over" (*begot* – "was the father of". *Villain* is used in two distinct senses: Oliver's *villain* in line 44 means "wicked fellow").

32 *railed on* – "spoken evil against".

33 *for your . . . accord* – "for the sake of your memory of your father, agree together".

34 *such exercises . . . gentleman* – "the training which it is proper for a gentleman to have". (In Shakespeare's time there was a clear division between the members of noble families and other people. This was reflected in the training a person received, and there were certain things that all gentlemen were expected to know or to be able to do.)

35 *allottery* – "share of money".

36 *buy my fortunes* – "to get myself a way of earning my living".

OLIVER

What, boy!   [*He strikes* ORLANDO

ORLANDO

Come, come, elder brother, you are too young[30] in this.

[*He seizes* OLIVER

OLIVER

Wilt thou lay hands on me, villain?

ORLANDO

I am no villain;[31] I am the youngest son of Sir Rowland de Boys; 45
he was my father, and he is thrice a villain that says such a father
begot villains. Wert thou not my brother, I would not take this
hand from thy throat till this other had pulled out thy tongue
for saying so. Thou hast railed[32] on thyself.

ADAM

Sweet masters, be patient; for your father's remembrance,[33] be 50
at accord.

OLIVER

Let me go, I say.

ORLANDO

I will not till I please: you shall hear me. My father charged
you in his will to give me good education: you have trained
me like a peasant, obscuring and hiding from me all gentle- 55
manlike qualities. The spirit of my father grows strong in me,
and I will no longer endure it. Therefore allow me such exercises[34] as may become a gentleman, or give me the poor allottery[35]
my father left me by testament; with that I will go buy my
fortunes.[36]   60

5

37 *your will* – "what is left to you by the 'will' you talk about". (The audience would see a second meaning: *have . . . your will* – "have part of what you want".)

38 *becomes me* – "is necessary", "suits me".

39 *Get you* – "Go away".

40 *lost my teeth* – "become old". (Adam supposes that he is no longer useful, like a dog that has lost its teeth in old age, but he has given his life to serving the de Boys family.)

41 *Is it even so* – "This is the situation, is it".

42 *grow upon me* – "grow like a sore on me". (There is a second meaning: the boy is growing up and growing too big.)

43 *physic your rankness* – "give you medicine to stop your quick growth *(rankness)*".

44 *give no . . . neither* – "and still not give you your thousand crowns" *(neither* – "either"; the "double negative" was common).

45 *Calls your worship* – "Are you calling (for me) sir" (*your worship*, "you" to a person of higher rank).

46 *So please you* – "If you please".

47 *importunes . . . you* – "begs to be allowed (to come in – *access*) to see you".

OLIVER

And what wilt thou do? Beg, when that is spent? Well, sir, get
you in. I will not long be troubled with you; you shall have some
part of your will.[37] I pray you leave me.

ORLANDO

I will no further offend you than becomes me[38] for my good.

OLIVER

Get you[39] with him, you old dog.   65

ADAM

Is "old dog" my reward? Most true, I have lost my teeth[40] in
your service. God be with my old master; he would not have
spoke such a word.
                    [*Exeunt* ORLANDO *and* ADAM

OLIVER

Is 't even[41] so? Begin you to grow[42] upon me? I will physic[43]
your rankness, and yet give no[44] thousand crowns neither.   70
Holla, Dennis!

Enter DENNIS

DENNIS

Calls[45] your worship?

OLIVER

Was not Charles, the Duke's wrestler, here to speak with me?

DENNIS

So please[46] you, he is here at the door and importunes[47] access
to you.   75

OLIVER

Call him in. [*Exit* DENNIS] 'T will be a good way; and tomorrow the wrestling is.

7

48 *morrow* – "morning".
49 *Monsieur* – "Master, Mr" (French).
50 *the new court*, i.e. the court under its new ruler.
51 *loving lords*, i.e. lords who love the old Duke and are loyal to him.
52 *revenues* – "receipts from rent" (these would be taken by the ruling Duke in their absence).
53 *good leave* – "full permission".
54 *being ever . . . together* – "because they have been brought up together, ever since they were babies" (*cradle*, a small bed for a baby).
55 *followed . . . behind her* – "followed her (Rosalind) into exile, or else she would have died because of being forced to stay behind".

56 *Robin Hood*, a famous rebel leader in the Middle Ages, who lived with his followers in hiding in Sherwood Forest, near Nottingham; many stories were told by country people about his adventures.
57 *fleet the time* – "make the time pass".
58 *golden world*, i.e. the world in the "golden age" of the past, as described by the poets, when men lived a simple, happy life in the open air (see Introduction, p. xix).

the old Robin Hood[56] *of England*

8

Enter CHARLES

CHARLES

Good morrow[48] to your worship.

OLIVER

Good Monsieur[49] Charles, what 's the new news at the new[50]
court?   80

CHARLES

There 's no news at the court, sir, but the old news; that is, the
old Duke is banished by his younger brother the new Duke, and
three or four loving[51] lords have put themselves into voluntary
exile with him, whose lands and revenues[52] enrich the new
Duke; therefore he gives them good leave[53] to wander.   85

OLIVER

Can you tell if Rosalind, the Duke's daughter, be banished with
her father?

CHARLES

O, no; for the Duke's daughter, her cousin, so loves her, being
ever[54] from their cradles bred together, that she would have
followed her exile,[55] or have died to stay behind her. She is at   90
the court, and no less beloved of her uncle than his own daughter;
and never two ladies loved as they do.

OLIVER

Where will the old Duke live?

CHARLES

They say he is already in the Forest of Arden, and a many merry
men with him; and there they live like the old Robin Hood[56]   95
of England. They say many young gentlemen flock to him
every day, and fleet[57] the time carelessly as they did in the
golden world.[58]

9

59 *What* – "It is true, is it, that".

60 *Marry, do I* – "Yes, I do indeed".

61 *I am given . . . understand* – "I have been told in secret".

62 *hath a disposition* – "intends".

63 *try a fall* – "see whether he can beat me". (A *fall*, when one wrestler was thrown down and could not get up, was the end of a match.)

64 *credit* – "reputation".

65 *shall acquit him well* – "will have shown that he is very good (as a wrestler)".

66 *for your love* – "for your sake".

67 *foil him* – "throw him violently".

68 *acquaint you withal* – "tell you about this".

69 *stay . . . intendment* – "prevent him from doing what he intends to do".

70 *brook* – "bear".

71 *of his own search* – "which he himself seeks".

72 *purpose herein* – "intention to do this".

73 *by underhand means* – "privately".

74 *an envious . . . parts* – "a man who hates *(envious)* the good qualities *(parts)* in other people and makes himself their rival *(emulator)*".

75 *contriver* – "plotter".

76 *natural brother* – "brother by birth" (and so his closest relative).

77 *I had . . . finger* – "I should be just as pleased if you broke his neck as if you broke his finger".

78 *thou wert . . . to 't* – "you had better take care", "you would be well advised to look after your own interests".

79 *mightily . . . on thee* – "gain great honour *(grace himself)* from fighting you".

80 *practise . . . poison* – "attempt to poison you secretly".

81 *entrap . . . device* – "catch you by some deceiving plot".

82 *but brotherly* – "only like a brother", i.e. as kindly as possible.

83 *should I . . . I must* – "if I described him to you in detail *(anatomise,* lay open like a body cut open for study) as he really is, it would make me".

OLIVER

What,[59] you wrestle tomorrow before the new Duke?

CHARLES

Marry, do I,[60] sir; and I came to acquaint you with a matter. I   100
am given,[61] sir, secretly to understand that your younger
brother, Orlando, hath a disposition[62] to come in disguised
against me to try a fall.[63] Tomorrow, sir, I wrestle for my
credit;[64] and he that escapes me without some broken limb shall
acquit[65] him well. Your brother is but young and tender, and,   105
for your love,[66] I would be loath to foil[67] him, as I must for my
own honour if he come in. Therefore, out of my love to you, I
came hither to acquaint[68] you withal, that either you might
stay[69] him from his intendment, or brook[70] such disgrace well
as he shall run into, in that it is a thing of his own search[71] and   110
altogether against my will.

OLIVER

Charles, I thank thee for thy love to me, which thou shalt find
I will most kindly requite. I had myself notice of my brother's
purpose herein,[72] and have by underhand[73] means laboured to
dissuade him from it, but he is resolute. I 'll tell thee, Charles,   115
it is the stubbornest young fellow of France; full of ambition,
an envious emulator[74] of every man's good parts, a secret and
villainous contriver[75] against me his natural[76] brother. Therefore use thy discretion: I had as lief[77] thou didst break his neck
as his finger. And thou wert best[78] look to 't; for if thou dost   120
him any slight disgrace, or if he do not mightily[79] grace himself on thee, he will practise[80] against thee by poison, entrap[81]
thee by some treacherous device, and never leave thee till
he hath ta'en thy life by some indirect means or other; for,
I assure thee – and almost with tears I speak it – there is not   125
one so young and so villainous this day living. I speak but
brotherly[82] of him, but should I anatomise[83] him to thee as
he is, I must blush and weep, and thou must look pale and
wonder.

11

84 *his payment* – "what he deserves", i.e. punishment.
85 *go alone again* – "goes back *(again)* without help".
86 *stir this gamester* – "encourage this sportsman" (to make sure that he will wrestle with Charles). Oliver is speaking to himself.
87 *gentle* – "noble in behaviour".
88 *device* – "ways of thinking".
89 *of all sorts . . . beloved* – "loved by people of all classes *(sorts)* just as if they were charmed".

90 *in the heart of* – "loved by".
91 *misprised* – "underrated, not respected".
92 *clear all* – "settle everything".
93 *kindle...thither* – "encourage *(kindle*, set fire to) the boy to go there *(thither)*".
94 *go about* – "attend to".

(I.ii) At the Court, Rosalind, Duke Senior's daughter, and Celia, the daughter of Duke Frederick, talk about the workings of Fortune and Nature. Touchstone, the clown or "fool", joins them. The wrestling match results in the defeat of Charles by Orlando. Orlando and Rosalind fall in love, and she gives him a chain to wear round his neck. It becomes clear that Sir Rowland, Orlando's father, used to be a close friend of Duke Senior.

1 *sweet my coz* – "my dear cousin" (*coz*, a shortened, affectionate form of "cousin").
2 *merry* – "cheerful".
3 *more mirth . . . merrier* – "more cheerfulness than I really feel (*am mistress of*, own); do you want me to be more cheerful than that".
4 *learn . . . pleasure* – "try to teach me to show more pleasure than is natural" (*remember* – "learn", as one learns a lesson by adding it to one's memory). Rosalind uses a metaphor (see Introduction, p. xxiv) from the schoolroom.

5 *Herein* – "In this (that you say)".
6 *so thou hadst* – "if you had".
7 *taught . . . for mine* – "trained my feelings *(taught my love)* to love your father as if he were my own father".
8 *So wouldst thou*, i.e. you would have loved my father as if he were your own.
9 *if the truth . . . thee* – "if your love were true, being made up of such right qualities as is my love to you".

CHARLES

I am heartily glad I came hither to you. If he come tomorrow, 130
I 'll give him his payment.[84] If ever he go alone[85] again, I 'll never
wrestle for prize more. And so, God keep your worship.

OLIVER

Farewell, good Charles. [*Exit* CHARLES] Now will I stir[86] this
gamester. I hope I shall see an end of him; for my soul, yet I
know not why, hates nothing more than he. Yet he 's gentle:[87] 135
never schooled and yet learned; full of noble device;[88] of all
sorts[89] enchantingly beloved; and indeed so much in the heart[90]
of the world, and especially of my own people, who best know
him, that I am altogether misprised.[91] But it shall not be so long;
this wrestler shall clear all.[92] Nothing remains but that I kindle 140
the boy thither,[93] which now I 'll go about.[94]

[*Exit*

Scene II. A level piece of grass near the Duke's palace.

Enter ROSALIND *and* CELIA.

CELIA

I pray thee, Rosalind, sweet my coz,[1] be merry.[2]

ROSALIND

Dear Celia, I show more mirth[3] than I am mistress of, and would
you yet I were merrier? Unless you could teach me to forget a
banished father, you must not learn[4] me how to remember any
extraordinary pleasure.   5

CELIA

Herein[5] I see thou lovest me not with the full weight that I love
thee. If my uncle, thy banished father, had banished thy uncle,
the Duke my father, so[6] thou hadst been still with me, I could
have taught my love[7] to take thy father for mine. So wouldst
thou,[8] if the truth of thy love to me were so righteously tem- 10
pered[9] as mine is to thee.

13

10 *the condition . . . estate* – "the state of my affairs", i.e. Rosalind will stop thinking about what has happened to herself, and she will be glad that Celia is fortunate.

11 *nor none . . . have* – "and is unlikely to have any (other children)".

12 *perforce* – "by force".

13 *render . . . affection* – "give back *(again)* to you because of my love".

14 *turn monster* – "become unnatural in shape and size".

15 *Rose*, a shorter form of *Rosalind*.

16 *devise sports* – "plan entertainments".

17 *to make . . . withal* – "(just) to amuse ourselves with it".

18 *in good earnest* – "seriously".

19 *nor no further . . . off again* – "and do not involve yourself even for amusement beyond the point at which you can withdraw *(come off again)* with an innocent girl's reddening of the face *(pure blush)* but no loss of reputation *(honour)*".

20 *mock . . . wheel* – "make fun of Fortune until we drive her away from her spinning-wheel". Ancient writers described Fortune as a goddess with a spinning-wheel like the wheel used by a married woman *(housewife)* to make thread; but Fortune's wheel produced good luck and success for some men, bad luck for others – these were the *gifts* of Fortune. If they drive Fortune away, Celia says, men's luck will be shared out *(bestowed)* more fairly after that *(henceforth)*.

21 *would* – "wish".

22 *mightily misplaced* – "given far too often to the wrong people".

23 *the bountiful blind woman*, i.e. Fortune, the generous *(bountiful)* goddess usually described as having her eyes covered (and so unable to see who receives her gifts).

24 *fair . . . ill-favouredly* – "beautiful, she very seldom makes virtuous *(honest)*; and those that she makes virtuous, she makes very ugly-looking".

the good housewife Fortune

14

ROSALIND

Well, I will forget the condition of my estate[10] to rejoice in yours.

CELIA

You know my father hath no child but I, nor none[11] is like to have, and truly, when he dies, thou shalt be his heir; for what he hath taken away from thy father perforce,[12] I will render[13] thee again in affection. By mine honour, I will, and when I break that oath, let me turn monster.[14] Therefore, my sweet Rose,[15] my dear Rose, be merry.

ROSALIND

From henceforth I will, coz, and devise sports.[16] Let me see; what think you of falling in love?

CELIA

Marry, I prithee, do, to make sport withal;[17] but love no man in good earnest,[18] nor no further[19] in sport, neither, than with safety of a pure blush thou mayst in honour come off again.

ROSALIND

What shall be our sport, then?

CELIA

Let us sit and mock the good housewife[20] Fortune from her wheel, that her gifts may henceforth be bestowed equally.

ROSALIND

I would[21] we could do so; for her benefits are mightily[22] misplaced; and the bountiful[23] blind woman doth most mistake in her gifts to women.

CELIA

'T is true, for those that she makes fair[24] she scarce makes honest, and those that she makes honest she makes very illfavouredly.

15

25 *thou goest . . . Nature's* – "you are not speaking now about Fortune's powers *(office)*, but Nature's". Rosalind refers to the idea that beauty and cleverness are natural, while money and our position among men (the *gifts of the world*, line 35) are matters of fortune, i.e. luck or chance.

26 *lineaments of Nature* – "the kind of face Nature gave us".

27 *No? . . . argument:* Celia argues that Fortune is more powerful than Nature: though Nature may make a person beautiful, Fortune can still make that person get into trouble *(fall into the fire* – the idea that a fall into the fire can spoil a person's beauty is also in the words). Nature, she continues, gave them (Rosalind and herself) enough good sense *(wit)* to mock at *(flout)* Fortune, but Fortune replies by sending Touchstone *(this fool,* whom she can see approaching) to bring the argument to an end.

28 *hard* – "clever".

29 *Nature's natural:* Fools were called *naturals,* i.e. children of nature.

30 *Peradventure* – "Perhaps".

31 *perceiveth . . . whetstone* – "has seen that the brains given to us by nature are not sharp enough for us to talk sensibly about Fortune and Nature *(these goddesses)* and so has sent this fool for us to sharpen them on" *(dull* – "blunt" as a knife may be when it needs sharpening, or *whetting,* on a stone used for that purpose; the fool is a *whetstone* in the sense that, by making fun of him, people can give practice to – and so, sharpen – their brains).

32 *How now . . . you* – "Hullo, clever man! Where are you going?" (Celia plays with two meanings of *wit:* she ironically calls the fool a "clever man", and at the same time she asks where his thoughts *(wit)* have wandered to (i.e. what is in his mind).

33 *messenger:* There are two ideas here: a *messenger* can be simply one who has been given a message, but the word was also used for a kind of police officer; Touchstone has not spoken as a servant speaks to the Duke's daughter, and her question refers to this.

34 *I was bid* – "I was ordered".

35 *that oath,* i.e. *by mine* (my) *honour.* Fools were not supposed to have any honour, but knights were generally considered honourable men. Touchstone's story of the knight and the pancakes (lines 52–5) shows in an amusing way that such beliefs about honour were mistaken, especially at Duke Frederick's court.

ROSALIND

Nay, now thou goest[25] from Fortune's office to Nature's. Fortune reigns in gifts of the world, not in the lineaments[26] of Nature. 35

Enter TOUCHSTONE, *the Clown.*

CELIA

No?[27] when Nature hath made a fair creature, may she not by Fortune fall into the fire? Though Nature hath given us wit to flout at Fortune, hath not Fortune sent in this fool to cut off the argument? 40

ROSALIND

Indeed, there is Fortune too hard[28] for Nature, when Fortune makes Nature's natural[29] the cutter-off of Nature's wit.

CELIA

Peradventure[30] this is not Fortune's work neither, but Nature's, who perceiveth[31] our natural wits too dull to reason of such goddesses, and hath sent this natural for our whetstone; for 45 always the dullness of the fool is the whetstone of the wits. How now,[32] wit; whither wander you?

TOUCHSTONE

Mistress, you must come away to your father.

CELIA

Were you made the messenger?[33]

TOUCHSTONE

No, by mine honour; but I was bid to come for you. 50

ROSALIND

Where learned you that oath,[35] fool?

17

36 *naught* – "bad" (also line 54).

37 *stand to it* – "keep to my opinion".

38 *was not . . . forsworn* – "had not lost his honour by swearing falsely by it". If a gentleman *swore* to (declared the truth of) a statement, he expected to be believed. If he swore to a statement knowing it to be untrue, he was *forsworn* and disgraced.

39 *heap* – "store".

40 *unmuzzle* – "let us hear" (a *muzzle* was a leather fastening round a dog's mouth; to *unmuzzle* was to set free).

41 *that that is not* – "something that does not exist" (their beards, because they are girls).

42 *you are not forsworn* – "you have not sworn falsely by it".

43 *who . . . meanest* – "which knight are you referring to".

44 *One that* – "Any knight whom".

45 *taxation* – "insulting remarks". (Touchstone has really said that Duke Frederick's knights are without honour.)

TOUCHSTONE

Of a certain knight that swore by his honour they were good
pancakes, and swore by his honour the mustard was naught.[36]
Now I 'll stand to it,[37] the pancakes were naught, and the mustard
was good, and yet was not the knight forsworn.[38]   55

CELIA

How prove you that, in the great heap[39] of your knowledge?

ROSALIND

Ay, marry, now unmuzzle[40] your wisdom.

TOUCHSTONE

Stand you both forth now: stroke your chins, and swear by your
beards that I am a knave.

CELIA

By our beards (if we had them) thou art.   60

TOUCHSTONE

By my knavery (if I had it) then I were; but if you swear by
that that is not,[41] you are not forsworn.[42] No more was this
knight, swearing by his honour, for he never had any; or if he
had, he had sworn it away before ever he saw those pancakes or
that mustard.   65

CELIA

Prithee, who is 't that thou meanest?[43]

TOUCHSTONE

One that[44] old Frederick, your father, loves.

CELIA

My father's love is enough to honour him. Enough! speak no
more of him; you 'll be whipped for taxation[45] one of these days.

46 *The more pity* – "It is a great pity,
    then,".
47 *what . . . foolishly* – "about the foolish
    things done by men who are be-
    lieved to be wise".
48 *By my troth* – "Indeed" (By my
    faith).
49 *since the little . . . show* – "since
    the small amount of good sense in
    fools was not allowed to make itself
    heard *(silenced)*, the small amount of
    foolishness in wise men is shown up
    very clearly".
50 *Le Beau* is a French family name; it
    also has a meaning, "The Fine
    (man)", which suggests the fashion-
    ably-dressed courtier.
51 *put on us . . . young* – "force us to
    receive, just as pigeons (doves) feed
    their young ones (by forcing food
    into their mouths)".
52 *news-crammed* – "filled with news".
    (Rosalind remembers an expression,
    "corn-crammed", used when a bird
    had corn forced into its crop, or
    lower food passage, to make it weigh
    more in the market.)

53 *marketable* – "easily sold at the
    market" (like the birds, but playing
    also with the idea of more easily
    finding a husband).
54 *Bon jour* – "Good day" (French).
55 *lost* – "missed".
56 *Sport? . . . colour?* – "What kind of
    sport". (There may be word-play
    on *colour*, because *sport* was pro-
    nounced rather like *spot*, which was
    a kind of ornamental stitching with
    coloured thread.)
57 *As wit . . . will* – "As your good
    sense – or mere chance – may decide
    to make you answer" (it is the ques-
    tion of Nature or Fortune again).

TOUCHSTONE

The more pity[46] that fools may not speak wisely what wise men 70
do foolishly.[47]

CELIA

By my troth,[48] thou sayest true; for since the little wit that fools
have was silenced,[49] the little foolery that wise men have makes
a great show. Here comes Monsieur le Beau.[50]

Enter LE BEAU

ROSALIND

With his mouth full of news. 75

CELIA

Which he will put[51] on us, as pigeons feed their young.

ROSALIND

Then shall we be news-crammed.[52]

CELIA

All the better; we shall be the more marketable.[53] Bon jour,[54]
Monsieur Le Beau, what 's the news?

LE BEAU

Fair princess, you have lost[55] much good sport. 80

CELIA

Sport?[56] Of what colour?

LE BEAU

What colour, madam? How shall I answer you?

ROSALIND

As wit and fortune[57] will.

21

58 *the Destinies decree* – "the powers or gods that control men's fortune give the order".

59 *laid . . . trowel* – "said in splendid language" (*laid on* – "spread thickly"; *trowel*, a tool to spread mortar, a builder's mixture of lime, sand, and water). The two girls and Touchstone are still making fun of Le Beau, and Touchstone's high-sounding words were probably a good imitation of the self-important courtier.

60 *Nay . . . rank* – "No, if I do not behave in the proper way for a man of my class" (Touchstone pretends to be offended by the suggestion that fine language does not come naturally from him).

61 *old smell* – "familiar smell". (Touchstone's word, *rank*, had two meanings: (i) class, and (ii) strong-smelling.)

62 *amaze* – "are confusing".

63 *lost the sight of* – "missed seeing".

64 *yet to do* – "still to happen".

65 *the beginning . . . buried* – "tell us about the beginning, which is all over".

66 *match . . . tale* – "tell another old story with the same beginning" (a very common beginning for such stories).

67 *proper . . . presence* – "good-looking *(proper)* young men of very good height and appearance *(presence)*".

TOUCHSTONE

Or as the Destinies[58] decree.

CELIA

Well said; that was laid on with a trowel.[59]   85

TOUCHSTONE

Nay, if I keep not my rank –[60]

ROSALIND

Thou losest thy old smell.[61]

LE BEAU

You amaze[62] me, ladies. I would have told you of good wrestling, which you have lost the sight of.[63]

ROSALIND

Yet tell us the manner of the wrestling.   90

LE BEAU

I will tell you the beginning; and if it please your ladyships, you may see the end; for the best is yet to do,[64] and here, where you are, they are coming to perform it.

CELIA

Well, the beginning,[65] that is dead and buried?

LE BEAU

There comes an old man and his three sons –   95

CELIA

I could match this beginning with an old tale.[66]

LE BEAU

Three proper[67] young men, of excellent growth and presence.

23

68 *bills* – "notices".

69 *Be it known . . . presents:* These were the first words of official notices. Rosalind is reminded of them by Le Beau's high-sounding statement ending with the word *presence*, but in the notices the words *by these presents* meant "by these writings which are present".

70 *which Charles . . . threw him* – "Charles very quickly threw him (to the ground)".

71 *that* – "so that".

72 *So he served* – "In the same way he treated".

73 *dole* – "expressions of grief".

74 *all . . . weeping* – "all that see him *(beholders)* show their sympathy *(take his part)* by weeping themselves".

75 *Thus . . . every day*, i.e. there is always something new to learn (said ironically).

76 *promise* – "declare (to)".

77 *any else . . . sides* – "anybody else who is anxious to see his own ribs broken". (There is word-play on *broken music*, which meant music arranged to be played by several persons in turn.)

78 *dotes upon* – "loves".

the place appointed for the wrestling

ROSALIND

With bills[68] on their necks. "Be it known[69] unto all men by
these presents."

LE BEAU

The eldest of the three wrestled with Charles, the Duke's 100
wrestler; which [70] Charles in a moment threw him and broke
three of his ribs, that[71] there is little hope of life in him. So he
served[72] the second, and so the third. Yonder they lie, the poor
old man, their father, making such pitiful dole[73] over them that
all the beholders[74] take his part with weeping.   105

ROSALIND

Alas!

TOUCHSTONE

But what is the sport, monsieur, that the ladies have lost?

LE BEAU

Why, this that I speak of.

TOUCHSTONE

Thus men may grow wiser[75] every day. It is the first time that
ever I heard breaking of ribs was sport for ladies.   110

CELIA

Or I, I promise[76] thee.

ROSALIND

But is there any else[77] longs to see this broken music in his sides?
Is there yet another dotes[78] upon rib-breaking? Shall we see this
wrestling, cousin?

LE BEAU

You must, if you stay here; for here is the place appointed for 115
the wrestling, and they are ready to perform it.

25

79 *Flourish*, a special trumpet call to proclaim the entrance of the ruler (Duke Frederick).

80 *entreated* – "persuaded" (to withdraw from the match).

81 *his own . . . forwardness* – "let his bold behaviour *(forwardness)* be at his own risk *(peril)*".

82 *successfully* – "able to succeed".

83 *How now* – "Hullo".

84 *Are you crept* – "Have you come quietly".

85 *my liege* – "my lord" (the usual way of addressing a ruler).

86 *so please . . . leave* – "if you will be kind enough to give us permission".

87 *there is such . . . man* – "the man (Charles – not the youth, Orlando) has such an advantage".

88 *fain* – "gladly".

89 *move* – "influence".

CELIA

Yonder, sure, they are coming. Let us now stay and see it.

Flourish.[79] *Enter* DUKE FREDERICK, LORDS, ORLANDO,
CHARLES, *and Attendants*

DUKE FREDERICK

Come on; since the youth will not be entreated,[80] his own
peril[81] on his forwardness.

ROSALIND

Is yonder the man?   120

LE BEAU

Even he, madam.

CELIA

Alas, he is too young! yet he looks successfully.[82]

DUKE FREDERICK

How now,[83] daughter and cousin! Are you crept[84] hither to see
the wrestling?

ROSALIND

Ay, my liege,[85] so please[86] you give us leave.   125

DUKE FREDERICK

You will take little delight in it, I can tell you, there is such odds[87]
in the man. In pity of the challenger's youth I would fain[88] dissuade him, but he will not be entreated. Speak to him, ladies;
see if you can move[89] him.

CELIA

Call him hither, good Monsieur Le Beau.   130

DUKE FREDERICK

Do so. I 'll not be by.   [*He moves away*

27

90 *them*, i.e. the two princesses (although Le Beau, who supports Duke Frederick, has said "the princess").

91 *the general challenger:* Charles has offered to fight all comers, and Orlando has, like others, accepted the offer; he has not demanded that Charles should fight him, as Le Beau suggested in calling Orlando "the challenger" (line 132).

92 *if you saw . . . enterprise* – "if you could see yourself or judge your own strength (in comparison with his), the realisation of the danger of what you are doing would advise *(counsel)* you to try your strength where you have a fairer chance".

93 *embrace* – "hold on to".

94 *shall not . . . misprised* – "will not be wrongly valued because of it (giving up the match)".

95 *suit* – "request".

96 *go forward* – "proceed" (in this way they will save Orlando from being shamed in public).

97 *punish . . . confess me* – "do not make me suffer by thinking badly of me, although I admit that I am". (Orlando's polite and modest way of speaking shows the nobility of his character in spite of his lack of education.)

98 *trial* – "test of strength".

99 *wherein . . . gracious* – "if I am defeated *(foiled)* in it, the disgrace is only for a man who was never in favour *(gracious)*" (so the shame of defeat will be slight).

100 *the world no injury* – "I shall have done the world no harm (by being killed)".

101 *Only in . . . supplied* – "In the world I only hold a place which may be filled by a better man".

LE BEAU

Monsieur the challenger, the princess calls for you.

ORLANDO

I attend them[90] with all respect and duty.

ROSALIND

Young man, have you challenged Charles the wrestler?

ORLANDO

No, fair princess; he is the general[91] challenger. I come but in 135
as others do, to try with him the strength of my youth.

CELIA

Young gentleman, your spirits are too bold for your years. You
have seen cruel proof of this man's strength; if you saw yourself
with your eyes,[92] or knew yourself with your judgment, the fear
of your adventure would counsel you to a more equal enterprise. 140
We pray you, for your own sake, to embrace[93] your own safety
and give over this attempt.

ROSALIND

Do, young sir. Your reputation shall not therefore be misprised:[94] we will make it our suit[95] to the Duke that the wrestling
might not go forward.[96]   145

ORLANDO

I beseech you, punish me not[97] with your hard thoughts, wherein
I confess me much guilty to deny so fair and excellent ladies
anything. But let your fair eyes and gentle wishes go with me
to my trial,[98] wherein if I be foiled,[99] there is but one shamed
that was never gracious; if killed, but one dead that is willing to 150
be so. I shall do my friends no wrong, for I have none to lament
me; the world[100] no injury, for in it I have nothing. Only in the
world I[101] fill up a place, which may be better supplied when I
have made it empty.

102 *would* – "wish".

103 *Pray . . . in you* – "I pray that I may be mistaken in what I think are your chances of success".

104 *gallant . . . earth* – "brave fellow who is so eager to be killed" (and then buried in the earth from which we all come).

105 *his will . . . working* – "his desire is more modest than that" (it is not his hope to be killed).

106 *try but one fall* – "wrestle only until one of you is thrown down for the first time".

107 *warrant* – "assure, promise".

108 *you shall not . . . first,* i.e. although the Duke persuaded Orlando so earnestly not to fight at all, there will be no need to beg him to avoid a second "round" (because, Charles means, the first throw will injure Orlando so much).

109 *You mean . . . before* – "If you intend to mock me after the fight, it is unwise (or unfair) to mock me before it".

110 *come your ways* – "come on"; "let us begin".

111 *Hercules . . . speed* – "may Hercules give you success *(speed)*". In ancient Greek literature, Hercules (or Herakles) was the strongest man in the world. Rosalind asks for Hercules to lend Orlando some of his strength.

ROSALIND

The little strength that I have, I would[102] it were with you.   155

CELIA

And mine, to eke out hers.

ROSALIND

Fare you well. Pray heaven[103] I be deceived in you!

CELIA

Your heart's desires be with you!

CHARLES

Come, where is this young gallant[104] that is so desirous to lie
with his mother earth?   160

ORLANDO

Ready, sir; but his will hath in it[105] a more modest working.

DUKE FREDERICK

You shall try but one fall.[106]

CHARLES

No, I warrant[107] your Grace you shall not entreat[108] him to a
second, that have so mightily persuaded him from a first.

ORLANDO

You mean[109] to mock me after; you should not have mocked 165
me before; but come your ways.[110]

ROSALIND

Now Hercules be thy speed,[111] young man!

CELIA

I would I were invisible, to catch the strong fellow by the leg.
                                        [*They wrestle*

31

112 *If I had . . . eye* – "Even if I were blind" (*thunderbolt*, a hard stone once believed to be hurled to earth by lightning).

113 *who should down* – "which of them will be thrown".

114 *I am . . . breathed* – "I have not had much exercise yet".

115 *How dost thou* – "How do you feel".

116 *I would . . . else* – "I wish you had been a different man's son."

117 *esteemed* – "considered".

118 *still* – "always".

119 *descended . . . house* – "been born a member of a different family". Orlando's father had been a supporter of Duke Senior; Duke Frederick wishes he had had a different father (*another father*, line 185).

120 *Were I my father* – "If I were in my father's place".

ROSALIND

O excellent young man!

CELIA

If I had a thunderbolt[112] in mine eye, I can tell who should 170
down.[113]
[A shout. CHARLES *is thrown*

DUKE FREDERICK

No more, no more.

ORLANDO

Yes, I beseech your Grace: I am not yet well breathed.[114]

DUKE FREDERICK

How dost[115] thou, Charles?

LE BEAU

He cannot speak, my lord.   175

DUKE FREDERICK

Bear him away. [CHARLES *is carried out*] What is thy name,
young man?

ORLANDO

Orlando, my liege, the youngest son of Sir Rowland de Boys.

DUKE FREDERICK

I would[116] thou hadst been son to some man else.
The world esteemed[117] thy father honourable,   180
But I did find him still[118] mine enemy.
Thou shouldst have better pleased me with this deed
Hadst thou descended from another house.[119]
But fare thee well; thou art a gallant youth:
I would thou hadst told me of another father.   185
[Exit DUKE *and Attendants*

CELIA

[*To* ROSALIND] Were I my father,[120] coz, would I do this?

33

121 *more proud*, i.e. than he would be if he had *another father* (line 185).

122 *calling* – "name".

123 *as his soul* – "as much as he loved himself".

124 *was of . . . mind* – "agreed with my father" (in loving Sir Rowland).

125 *his son* – "to be his son".

126 *I should . . . ventured* – "I would have added tears to my pleading before *(ere)* I let him take such a risk".

127 *Sticks me at heart*, i.e. grieves my heart as if a knife were stuck there.

128 *But justly . . . promise* – "as perfectly as (in your wrestling) you have performed much more than all you promised".

129 *for me . . . fortune* – "as a sign of friendship, from someone who is not in the favour of fortune".
("In suit" meant "in service", since the Elizabethans dressed their servants in special suits of clothing. "Out of suits" therefore meant "dismissed", "not cared for". Fortune is personified.)

130 *That could . . . means* – "one (Rosalind herself) who would like to give more, but cannot because she has no more to give". (After saying this, Rosalind wants to go away – *Shall we go, coz?* she says to Celia – because she has fallen in love and is overcome by shyness.)

131 *My better . . . stands up* – "My good manners and qualities have been defeated, and the man who is standing here". (Orlando has fallen in love, too, and shyness has robbed him of the power to make fine speeches.)

132 *quintain*, a wooden figure of a man which horsemen attacked to practise their skill in fighting on horseback.

a quintain,[132] *a mere lifeless block*

ORLANDO

I am more proud[121] to be Sir Rowland's son,
His youngest son, and would not change that calling[122]
To be adopted heir to Frederick.

ROSALIND

[*To* CELIA] My father loved Sir Rowland as his soul,[123]   190
And all the world was of my father's mind.[124]
Had I before known this young man his son,[125]
I should have given him tears unto[126] entreaties,
Ere he should thus have ventured.

CELIA

　　　　[*To* ROSALIND] Gentle cousin,
Let us go thank him and encourage him: 195
My father's rough and envious disposition
Sticks[127] me at heart. [*To* ORLANDO] Sir, you have well
　　deserved;
If you do keep your promises in love
But justly[128] as you have exceeded all promise,
Your mistress shall be happy.

ROSALIND

　　　　　　　　Gentleman, [*giving him the chain*   200
　from round her neck]
Wear this for me, one out of suits[129] with fortune,
That could[130] give more, but that her hand lacks means.
Shall we go, coz?　　　　　　　　[*She turns and walks away*

CELIA [*Following*]

Ay. Fare you well, fair gentleman.

ORLANDO

Can I not say, "I thank you"? My better parts[131]   205
Are all thrown down, and that which here stands up
Is but a quintain,[132] a mere lifeless block.

133 *would* – "wants".

134 *overthrown . . . enemies* – "conquered others (i.e. your friends) besides your enemies". (He has "conquered" her heart. She does not clearly say so, but Celia thinks she is in danger of admitting her love, and in the next line asks her to leave: *Will you go, coz?* – "Let us go now".)

135 *Have with you* – "I am coming (with you)".

136 *hangs . . . tongue*, i.e. makes me unable to speak.

137 *urged conference* – "invited conversation".

138 *Or Charles . . . weaker* – "Either Charles or something not so strong as he", i.e. love of Rosalind.

139 *Albeit* – "Although".

140 *applause* – "approval".

141 *condition* – "state of mind".

142 *humorous* – "in a bad humour, bad-tempered".

143 *what he is . . . speak of* – "it is better for you to imagine *(conceive)* what he is like than for me to describe it". (As a courtier, Le Beau dare not speak openly of the Duke's terrible anger.)

144 *here was* – "was here".

ROSALIND

He calls us back. My pride fell with my fortunes;
I 'll ask him what he would.[133] [*She turns back*] Did you
   call, sir?
Sir, you have wrestled well, and overthrown[134]   210
More than your enemies.

CELIA

       Will you go, coz?

ROSALIND

Have with you.[135] Fare you well.

             [*Exeunt* ROSALIND *and* CELIA

ORLANDO

What passion hangs these weights[136] upon my tongue?
I cannot speak to her, yet she urged conference.[137]

Enter LE BEAU

O poor Orlando, thou art overthrown!   215
Or Charles[138] or something weaker masters thee.

LE BEAU

Good sir, I do in friendship counsel you
To leave this place. Albeit[139] you have deserved
High commendation, true applause,[140] and love,
Yet such is now the Duke's condition[141]   220
That he misconstrues all that you have done.
The Duke is humorous;[142] what he is, indeed,
More suits you to conceive[143] than I to speak of.

ORLANDO

I thank you, sir; and pray you, tell me this:
Which of the two was daughter of the Duke,   225
That here was[144] at the wrestling?

145 *Neither . . . manners:* Since both Rosalind and Celia show good manners, neither of them behaves like Duke Frederick's daughter.

146 *whose loves . . . sisters* – "their love for each other is deeper than it would be if they were sisters" (*natural bond*, the links with which nature binds sisters together).

147 *of late . . . But that* – "recently Duke Frederick has developed a dislike of his noble niece, with only one reason (*argument*) for it (his dislike) – that" (*ta'en* – "taken"; *'gainst* – "against"; *Grounded* – "based").

148 *suddenly break forth* – "very soon show itself".

149 *Hereafter* – "At some later time".

150 *world* – "state of society" (i.e. under the true Duke).

151 *I shall desire . . . of you* – "I hope to have you as a friend and to know you better".

152 *rest much bounden* – "remain very grateful".

153 *Thus must . . . smother* – "So now I must go away from one danger and into a greater danger". Orlando uses an Elizabethan expression (*smother* – "smoke which stops one's breathing") with a meaning similar to that of the modern expression, "out of the frying pan into the fire".

(I.iii) Rosalind speaks to Celia about her love for Orlando. Duke Frederick comes to them and angrily banishes Rosalind from the court. Celia decides to go with her, and they arrange for Rosalind to disguise herself as a boy, taking the name of Ganymede. Celia will pretend to be "Ganymede's" young sister, and Touchstone will go with them into Arden.

1 *Why,* said in an attempt to attract attention. Rosalind's thoughts are far away, and Celia cannot get an answer from her.

2 *Cupid,* the ancient god of love.

LE BEAU

Neither his daughter, if we judge by manners;[145]
But yet, indeed, the smaller is his daughter;
The other is daughter to the banished Duke,
And here detained by her usurping uncle   230
To keep his daughter company; whose loves[146]
Are dearer than the natural bond of sisters.
But I can tell you that of late[147] this Duke
Hath ta'en displeasure 'gainst his gentle niece,
Grounded upon no other argument   235
But that the people praise her for her virtues,
And pity her for her good father's sake;
And, on my life, his malice 'gainst the lady
Will suddenly[148] breath forth. Sir, fare you well.
Hereafter,[149] in a better world[150] than this,   240
I shall desire more love[151] and knowledge of you.

ORLANDO

I rest much bounden[152] to you: fare you well.

[*Exit* LE BEAU

Thus must I[153] from the smoke into the smother,
From tyrant Duke unto a tyrant brother.
But heavenly Rosalind!   [*Exit* 245

Scene III. The palace.
Enter CELIA *and* ROSALIND.

CELIA

Why,[1] cousin! Why, Rosalind! Cupid[2] have mercy, not a word?

ROSALIND

Not one to throw at a dog.

39

3 *lame me with reasons* – "throw some reasons (for your silence) at me to make me lame" (as if throwing stones at a dog).

4 *there were . . . laid up* – "there would be two injured *(laid up)* cousins".

5 *mad without any* – "overcome by sadness without a reason". Rosalind refers to herself.

6 *all this*, i.e. this silence and sadness.

7 *my child's father*, i.e. the man she would like to marry, who would then become the father of her child.

8 *how full . . . world* – "how many difficulties there are in this world of ordinary life" (*briers* – literally "thorny bushes").

9 *but burrs . . . foolery* – "only rough seed-cases thrown on your clothes in holiday fun", i.e. these troubles are only small annoyances. (A *burr* is the rough case of a seed; it fastens itself to clothes, and it was therefore a common holiday joke to throw burrs at people. There is a contrast in *briers – burrs, working-day world – holiday foolery*.)

10 *if we walk . . . paths*, i.e. if we do not follow the usual ways (it was not usual for princesses to talk to unknown wrestlers).

11 *Hem them away* – "Clear them away by coughing". (There is word-play on *burr* and a *bur* in the throat, a need to cough. *Hem* is the sound of a cough and it can also mean to turn up the edge of a garment – a petticoat for example.)

12 *cry . . . "him"* – "cough with the sound 'hem' and get 'him' (i.e. Orlando)".

13 *wrestle . . . affections* – "fight against your strong feelings".

14 *take the part of* – "are on the side of". (It is useless, Rosalind means, for her to struggle against her feelings because they are on Orlando's side, and he is a stronger wrestler.)

40

CELIA

No, thy words are too precious to be cast away upon curs; throw some of them at me; come, lame me with reasons.[3]

ROSALIND

Then there were two cousins laid up,[4] when the one should be   5
lamed with reasons, and the other mad[5] without any.

CELIA

But is all this[6] for your father?

ROSALIND

No, some of it is for my child's father.[7] O, how full of briers[8]
is this working-day world!

CELIA

They are but burrs,[9] cousin, thrown upon thee in holiday   10
foolery; if we walk not in the trodden paths,[10] our very petticoats will catch them.

ROSALIND

I could shake them off my coat; these burrs are in my heart.

CELIA

Hem[11] them away.

ROSALIND

I would try, if I could cry "hem", and have "him".[12]   15

CELIA

Come, come, wrestle with thy affections.[13]

ROSALIND

O, they take the part[14] of a better wrestler than myself.

41

15 *a good wish . . . fall* – "bless you. You will learn in time, even if you learn by being thrown by a stronger wrestler". (Celia repeats the idea of I.ii.210 that Orlando has "over-thrown" Rosalind's heart by his wrestling.)

16 *turning . . . service* – "let us finish joking". The image is of dismissing the jokes *(jests)* like servants who are no longer needed. Celia wants to end the word-play and talk seriously *(in good earnest)*.

17 *ensue* – "follow (in the way of reasoning)".

18 *chase* – "reasoning" (following from point to point).

19 *dearly* – "deeply".

20 *faith* – "indeed".

21 *Doth he . . . well:* Celia means that, if she behaved like her father (by *this kind of chase*, line 25), she should hate those who deserve well, and since Orlando deserves well, she should hate him.

22 *dispatch you . . . court* – "be as quick as you can, for your own safety, and leave the court".

CELIA

O, a good wish[15] upon you! You will try in time, in despite of
a fall. But turning these jests[16] out of service, let us talk in
good earnest. Is it possible, on such a sudden, you should   20
fall into so strong a liking with old Sir Rowland's youngest
son?

ROSALIND

The Duke my father loved his father dearly.

CELIA

Doth it therefore ensue[17] that you should love his son dearly?
By this kind of chase,[18] I should hate him, for my father hated   25
his father dearly;[19] yet I hate not Orlando.

ROSALIND

No, faith,[20] hate him not, for my sake.

CELIA

Why should I not? Doth he not deserve well?[21]

Enter DUKE FREDERICK *with Attendants*

ROSALIND

Let me love him for that, and do you love him because I do.
Look, here comes the Duke.   30

CELIA

With his eyes full of anger.

DUKE FREDERICK

Mistress, dispatch you[22] with your safest haste,
And get you from our court.

ROSALIND

Me, uncle?

43

23 *cousin* was often used by the Elizabethans in addressing any relative.

24 *if that thou beest* – "if you are".

25 *Let me . . . bear with me*, i.e. "Let me take with me the knowledge of what wrong I have done".

26 *If with . . . intelligence* – "If I have some understanding of myself".

27 *frantic* – "mad".

28 *a thought unborn* – "an idea before it has become a clear thought".

29 *Thus do all traitors* – "All traitors talk like that".

30 *If their . . . words* – "if (their own) words were enough to free them from suspicion".

31 *suffice thee* – "be sufficient (reason) for you".

32 *whereon . . . depends* – "what makes it likely that I am a traitor".

33 *derive . . . that to me* – "receive it (as an inheritance) from our relatives, how does that affect my case". (The reason for claiming that it does not affect her case is given in the next sentence: her father was not a traitor, so she has not inherited treason.)

34 *mistake . . . treacherous* – "do not make the mistake of thinking that being poor makes me a traitor".

DUKE FREDERICK

You, cousin,[23]
Within these ten days if that thou beest[24] found
So near our public court as twenty miles,   35
Thou diest for it.

ROSALIND

I do beseech your Grace,
Let me the knowledge[25] of my fault bear with me.
If with myself I hold intelligence,[26]
Or have acquaintance with mine own desires,
If that I do not dream or be not frantic –[27]   40
As I do trust I am not – then, dear uncle,
Never so much as in a thought unborn[28]
Did I offend your Highness.

DUKE FREDERICK

Thus do[29] all traitors:
If their purgation[30] did consist in words,
They are as innocent as grace itself.   45
Let it suffice[31] thee that I trust thee not.

ROSALIND

Yet your mistrust cannot make me a traitor.
Tell me whereon[32] the likelihood depends.

DUKE FREDERICK

Thou art thy father's daughter; there 's enough.

ROSALIND

So was I when your Highness took his dukedom;   50
So was I when your Highness banished him.
Treason is not inherited, my lord;
Or if we did derive[33] it from our friends,
What 's that to me? My father was no traitor.
Then, good my liege, mistake[34] me not so much   55
To think my poverty is treacherous.

45

35 *stayed her* – "kept her back".

36 *Else had . . . along* – "otherwise she would have gone wandering with her father".

37 *remorse* – "pity".

38 *still* – "always".

39 *Rose at an instant* – "(we) have always got up at the same moment".

40 *eat* – "eaten".

41 *like Juno's swans:* Juno, in the ancient Roman belief, was the wife of the god Jupiter. But Shakespeare seems to have made a mistake: it was Venus, the goddess of love, whose car was drawn through the sky by two swans.

42 *coupled* – "as a pair".

43 *subtle* – "deceiving".

44 *smoothness* – "gentle manner". Duke Frederick is a typical tyrant in his fear of the people he rules.

45 *she robs . . . name* – "she gets for herself the good name that you should have".

46 *open not thy lips* – "do not talk about it (any more)".

47 *doom* – "judgement and sentence".

48 *Pronounce . . . on me* – "Declare the same judgement and sentence on me".

49 *provide yourself* – "make your preparations".

50 *If you outstay . . . die* – "If you are still here after the given time (ten days), I swear by my honour – and with all the authority of my commands – that you shall be put to death".

CELIA

Dear sovereign, hear me speak.

DUKE FREDERICK

Ay, Celia; we stayed[35] her for your sake,
Else had she[36] with her father ranged along.

CELIA

I did not then entreat to have her stay;   60
It was your pleasure and your own remorse.[37]
I was too young that time to value her,
But now I know her. If she be a traitor,
Why, so am I; we still[38] have slept together,
Rose at an instant;[39] learned, played, eat[40] together;   65
And whereso'er we went, like Juno's[41] swans,
Still we went coupled[42] and inseparable.

DUKE FREDERICK

She is too subtle[43] for thee; and her smoothness,[44]
Her very silence and her patience
Speak to the people, and they pity her.   70
Thou art a fool: she robs thee of thy name,[45]
And thou wilt show more bright and seem more virtuous.
When she is gone. Then open[46] not thy lips:
Firm and irrevocable is my doom[47]
Which I have passed upon her; she is banished.   75

CELIA

Pronounce[48] that sentence then on me, my liege;
I cannot live out of her company.

DUKE FREDERICK

You are a fool. You, niece, provide yourself.[49]
If you outstay[50] the time, upon mine honour,
And in the greatness of my word, you die.   80
                    [*Exit* DUKE FREDERICK *and Attendants*

51 *change* – "exchange".

52 *charge thee* – "want you to promise".

53 *That he hath not* – "He has certainly not done that".

54 *Rosalind . . . am one* – "Then you cannot have such love for me as would make you see (understand) that you and I are one person".

55 *devise . . . fly* – "make a plan with me how we may run away".

56 *your change . . . me out* – "your changed circumstances alone, facing your own troubles alone, and not sharing them with me".

57 *now at . . . pale:* The sky, now it is evening, has turned pale – in sympathy, Celia says, with their unhappiness.

CELIA

O my poor Rosalind, whither wilt thou go?
Wilt thou change[51] fathers? I will give thee mine.
I charged[52] thee, be not thou more grieved than I am.

ROSALIND

I have more cause.

CELIA

          Thou hast not, cousin.
Prithee be cheerful: know'st thou not the Duke   85
Hath banished me, his daughter?

ROSALIND

          That he hath not.[53]

CELIA

No? Hath not? Rosalind lacks[54] then the love
Which teacheth thee that thou and I am one.
Shall we be sundered? Shall we part, sweet girl?
No; let my father seek another heir.   90
Therefore devise[55] with me how we may fly,
Whither to go, and what to bear with us;
And do not seek to take your change[56] upon you,
To bear your griefs yourself, and leave me out;
For, by this heaven, now at our sorrows pale,[57]   95
Say what thou canst, I 'll go along with thee.

ROSALIND

Why, whither shall we go?

CELIA

To seek my uncle in the Forest of Arden.

58 *Maids* – "young girls".

59 *mean attire . . . do you* (line 102) – "humble clothes *(attire)* and darken my face with a brown stain *(umber)*; you do the same". This, Celia thinks, will make them unattractive to strange men while travelling.

60 *Were it not . . . all points* – "Since I am unusually *(more than common)* tall, would it not be better for me to dress in every detail".

61 *a gallant curtle-axe* – "a good broad sword (hanging)". (The curtle-axe would hang at the side; it was a forester's sword – both weapon and wood-cutting edge.)

62 *in my heart . . . there will* – "whatever woman's fear may be hidden inside my heart".

63 *swashing* – "boastful".

64 *As many . . . semblances* – "just as a lot of cowards who are men in other ways make a bold pretence with an appearance of bravery". (Rosalind says that a good many men are not really brave but make a bold show and are therefore accepted as fearless; she too can put on a bold, soldier-like outside appearance to hide her woman's fear.)

65 *Jove's own page*, the boy attendant *(page)* of Jupiter *(Jove)*, the king of the Roman gods. This page's name was Ganymede; Shakespeare took the names *Ganymede* for Rosalind and *Aliena* for Celia (line 119) from Lodge's story, *Rosalynde* (see Introduction, p. viii) *(look you call* – "you must call").

66 *hath . . . my state* – "refers to my present condition" (as a wanderer – *Aliena* is Latin for "a stranger").

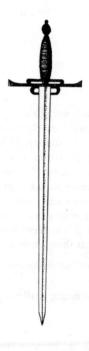

A gallant curtle-axe[61]

50

ROSALIND

Alas, what danger will it be to us,
Maids[58] as we are, to travel forth so far!   100
Beauty provoketh thieves sooner than gold.

CELIA

I 'll put myself in poor and mean[59] attire
And with a kind of umber smirch my face;
The like do you; so shall we pass along,
And never stir assailants.

ROSALIND

       Were it not[60] better,   105
Because that I am more than common tall,
That I did suit me all points like a man?
A gallant curtle-axe[61] upon my thigh,
A boar-spear in my hand; and – in my heart
Lie[62] there what hidden woman's fear there will –   110
We 'll have a swashing[63] and a martial outside,
As many other mannish[64] cowards have
That do outface it with their semblances.

CELIA

What shall I call thee when thou art a man?

ROSALIND

I 'll have no worse a name than Jove's[65] own page,   115
And therefore look you call me Ganymede.
But what will you be called?

CELIA

Something that hath a reference[66] to my state:
No longer Celia, but Aliena.

67 *what if we assayed* – "would it be a good idea if we attempted".

68 *The clownish fool* – "the simple fool", i.e. Touchstone. Many courts kept a so-called "fool" whose duty was to amuse the company (see Introduction, pp. xiv–v).

69 *comfort to our travel* – "protection for us on our travels".

70 *woo* – "persuade (him to join us)".

71 *Let 's away* – "Let us go now".

72 *go we in content* – "let us go calmly".

ROSALIND

But, cousin, what if we assayed[67] to steal   120
The clownish fool[68] out of your father's court?
Would he not be a comfort[69] to our travel?

CELIA

He 'll go along o'er the wide world with me;
Leave me alone to woo[70] him. Let 's[71] away,
And get our jewels and our wealth together;   125
Devise the fittest time and safest way
To hide us from pursuit that will be made
After my flight. Now go we in content[72]
To liberty, and not to banishment.

[*Exeunt*

(II.i) In the Forest of Arden, Duke Senior talks about the benefits of living close to nature and about "the uses of adversity". Jaques is described by the Fird Lord, who also gives an account of some of Jaques's opinions.

1 *Duke Senior:* The name means "the older duke"; it is used all through the play for Frederick's elder brother, the rightful duke.

2 *co-mates* – "companions".

3 *old custom* – "long habit", "a long time in which to get used to it".

4 *painted pomp* – "artificial ceremony" (as in a court).

5 *More . . . envious court:* The idea here is that at court there is always danger *(peril)* from jealous rivals who try to harm one so as to gain an advantage.

6 *Here feel . . . Adam* – "Do we not feel Adam's punishment here". According to the Bible, Adam, the first man, was driven out of the Garden of Eden for disobeying God. Eden was the garden of everlasting spring, and Adam's punishment included the change of weather from season to season *(the seasons' difference,* line 6). The idea of Eden was similar to that of the "Golden Age" as described by the Greek and Roman poets (see Introduction, p. xix).

7 *as* – "such as".

8 *icy fang . . . chiding* – "cold bite and cruel sound" (two images for the winter wind; *fang* – "sharp tooth of an animal"; *churlish* – "bad-mannered"; *chiding* – scolding noise).

9 *Which* – "at which".

10 *shrink* – "draw back" (trying to get away from the cold).

11 *feelingly . . . I am* – "make me see my true character through my feelings".

12 *Sweet . . . adversity* – "Bad fortune *(adversity)* brings valuable benefits *(uses)*".

13 *the toad . . . his head:* It was believed that the *toad* (a creature rather like a frog but with an ugly body usually covered with swellings) was poisonous *(venomous)* but had in its head the precious "toadstone", a remedy for poison.

14 *exempt . . . haunt* – "(in a place which is) free from the society of other people".

15 *tongues . . . stones* – "lessons to be learnt from (looking at) trees as if they could speak, brooks as if they were books to be read, and stones as if they preached good behaviour to us".

16 *translate . . . style* – "take the cruelty *(stubbornness)* of fortune and change it into so gentle and pleasant a way of looking at life" (*translate* has also its usual modern sense of changing into another language: Duke Senior is said to "translate" the cruelty of fortune in a pleasant "style".

17 *us* – "for ourselves".

18 *it irks . . . gored* – "it is painful to me that these poor harmless spotted creatures *(dappled fools)*, who are born citizens *(native burghers)* of this lonely state, should have their rounded backs wounded *(gored)* by arrows *(forked heads)* in their own country *(confines)*" *(dappled* – "marked with groups of lighter-coloured spots"; *haunches,* the parts – rounded in healthy deer – above the back legs). The Duke imagines the forest as a kind of city-state for the animals, and it does not seem fair that men, who are not *natives* of the state, should kill its citizens, even for food.

ACT II

Scene I. The Forest of Arden.

Enter DUKE SENIOR,[1] AMIENS, *and two or three Lords,*
dressed like foresters.

DUKE SENIOR

Now, my co-mates[2] and brothers in exile,
Hath not old custom[3] made this life more sweet
Than that of painted pomp?[4] Are not these woods
More free from peril than the envious[5] court?
Here feel we not[6] the penalty of Adam,   5
The seasons' difference; as[7] the icy fang[8]
And churlish chiding of the winter's wind,
Which,[9] when it bites and blows upon my body
Even till I shrink[10] with cold, I smile and say
"This is no flattery; these are counsellors   10
That feelingly[11] persuade me what I am."
Sweet are the uses[12] of adversity,
Which, like the toad,[13] ugly and venomous,
Wears yet a precious jewel in his head;
And this our life, exempt[14] from public haunt,   15
Finds tongues[15] in trees, books in the running brooks,
Sermons in stones, and good in everything.
I would not change it.

AMIENS

                     Happy is your Grace,
That can translate[16] the stubbornness of fortune
Into so quiet and so sweet a style.   20

DUKE SENIOR

Come, shall we go and kill us[17] venison?
And yet it irks[18] me the poor dappled fools,
Being native burghers of this desert city,

19 *Jaques* is pronounced with two syllables: "Jay-kis" or "Jay-quiz" [ˈdʒeikwiz].

20 *in that kind swears* – "in that matter (of hunting the deer) declares (that)".

21 *steal* – "move silently".

22 *along* – "at full length".

23 *antique* – "very old".

24 *brawls along* – "flows noisily (over stones) through".

25 *the which* – "which".

26 *sequestered* – "separated (from its companions)". The description of the wounded stag (male deer) forsaken by other deer brings out an important idea in the play. Nature is often cruel and pitiless, but no worse than men, who behave towards their poorer fellow-citizens just like the other deer to their suffering companion. (See Introduction, p. xv.) The style of the speech is rather artificial; this is to make the audience pay special attention to the "story within a story", not to suggest that Jacques's opinions at this point in the play are foolish.

27 *That from . . . a hurt* – "which had received a wound *(ta'en a hurt)* from the arrow aimed at it by the hunter".

28 *languish* – "die slowly".

29 *heaved . . . coat* – "gave such deep groans that as they came out they stretched its skin" *(discharge* – "letting (the groans) out"; *leathern* – "made of leather", as the skin of a deer is).

30 *Coursed one another* – "hurried one after another".

31 *piteous* – "stirring one's pity".

32 *hairy fool* – "dear creature *(fool)* in its coat of hair".

33 *much marked of* – "closely observed by".

34 *the extremest verge* – "the very edge (of the water)".

35 *Augmenting . . . tears* – "increasing (the amount of water in) it with its tears".

36 *moralise this spectacle* – "draw out the hidden meaning of this sight", or "draw moral lessons from this sight (i.e. lessons in right and wrong human behaviour)".

37 *for his . . . needless stream* – "about its crying (and dropping tears) into the stream which did not need the extra liquid *(needless)*".

38 *testament*, i.e. a will dividing up one's possessions after death.

39 *worldlings* – "men in the (human) world". Like rich men who leave money to those who already have too much, the stag was adding an extra amount *(sum of more)* to the stream which was already full of water.

40 *of his velvet friends* – "by his soft-coated friends", i.e. the other deer, but there is also a suggestion of the courtier's velvet suit.

41 *misery doth . . . company* – "poverty *(misery)* turns away the flow *(flux)* of visitors *(company)*".

Should, in their own confines, with forkéd heads
Have their round haunches gored.

FIRST LORD

                    Indeed, my lord,   25
The melancholy Jaques[19] grieves at that,
And in that kind[20] swears you do more usurp
Than doth your brother that hath banished you.
Today my Lord of Amiens and myself
Did steal[21] behind him as he lay along[22]   30
Under an oak whose antique[23] root peeps out
Upon the brook that brawls[24] along this wood;
To the which[25] place a poor sequestered[26] stag,
That from the hunter's aim[27] had ta'en a hurt,
Did come to languish;[28] and indeed, my lord,   35
The wretched animal heaved forth[29] such groans
That their discharge did stretch his leathern coat
Almost to bursting, and the big round tears
Coursed[30] one another down his innocent nose
In piteous[31] chase; and thus the hairy fool,[32]   40
Much markéd of[33] the melancholy Jaques,
Stood on the extremest[34] verge of the swift brook,
Augmenting[35] it with tears.

DUKE SENIOR

               But what said Jaques?
Did he not moralise[36] this spectacle?

FIRST LORD

O, yes, into a thousand similes.   45
First, for[37] his weeping into the needless stream:
"Poor deer," quoth he, "thou mak'st a testament[38]
As worldlings[39] do, giving thy sum of more
To that which had too much": then, being there alone,
Left and abandoned of his velvet friends:[40]   50
"'T is right," quoth he, "thus misery doth part[41]

42 *Anon . . . greet him* – "soon *(Anon)* a group *(herd)* of deer, not caring because they are full of the good field grass *(pasture)* that they have eaten, come jumping past him and do not stop *(never stays)* to take notice of him" (like well-fed citizens passing a poor man).

43 *Sweep on* – "Pass on without stopping".

44 *greasy* – "smooth and oily (like rich men)".

45 *the fashion* – "the usual way of things".

46 *wherefore . . . look upon* – "why should you look at".

47 *broken* – "ruined" (not able to get any money at all).

48 *most invectively . . . our life* – "with words of the sharpest condemnation he attacks *(pierceth through* suggests piercing with arrows) the people of the countryside, city and court; yes, and he attacks our (way of) life (here too)".

49 *mere* – "complete".

50 *what 's worse* – "even worse (than that)".

51 *kill them . . . place* – "kill them off in the place that was specially given to them *(assigned)* and where they were born *(native)*".

52 *cope* – "meet with".

53 *sullen fits* – "bitter states of mind".

54 *matter* – "serious thought".

55 *straight* – "immediately".

(II.ii) Duke Frederick finds out that Celia and Touchstone have escaped with Rosalind. He believes that Orlando is with them, and sends for Oliver.

1 *Are of consent . . . this* – "have agreed with this (escape) and have allowed it".

a poor sequestered[26] *stag,*
That from the hunter's aim had ta'en a hurt

The flux of company": anon a careless[42] herd,
Full of the pasture, jumps along by him
And never stays to greet him: "Ay," quoth Jaques,
"Sweep on,[43] you fat and greasy[44] citizens,   55
'T is just the fashion:[45] wherefore do you[46] look
Upon that poor and broken[47] bankrupt there?"
Thus most invectively he[48] pierceth through
The body of the country, city, court,
Yea, and of this our life; swearing that we   60
Are mere[49] usurpers, tyrants, and what 's worse,[50]
To fright the animals and to kill them up[51]
In their assigned and native dwelling place.

DUKE SENIOR

And did you leave him in this contemplation?

SECOND LORD

We did, my lord, weeping and commenting   65
Upon the sobbing deer.

DUKE SENIOR

           Show me the place.
I love to cope[52] him in these sullen fits,[53]
For then he 's full of matter.[54]

FIRST LORD

I 'll bring you to him straight.[55]   [*Exeunt*

Scene II. *The palace.*

Enter DUKE FREDERICK, *with Attendants.*

DUKE FREDERICK

Can it be possible that no man saw them?
It cannot be; some villains of my court
Are of consent[1] and sufferance in this.

59

2 *The ladies . . . a-bed* – "The ladies whose duty it is to assist her (Celia) in her bedroom *(chamber)* saw her in bed".

3 *untreasured of their mistress* – "empty of the treasure it should have contained – their lady".

4 *roynish* – "coarse".

5 *oft* – "often".

6 *was wont* – "used"; "was in the habit of (laughing)".

7 *gentlewoman* – "lady (acting as a servant to the princess)".

8 *parts and graces* – "good qualities of body and mind".

9 *but lately . . . Charles* – "so recently defeat Charles, the very strong man".

10 *gallant* – "fine fellow" (Orlando; the Duke calls him a *gallant* ironically).

11 *suddenly* – "at once".

12 *let not . . . quail* – "the searching and enquiries *(inquisition)* must not be given up" (*quail* – literally, "give way out of fear").

13 *again* – "back".

(II.iii) Returning to his home, Orlando is met by Adam and warned that Oliver is again plotting to kill him. Orlando decides to run away, and the faithful old servant offers to go with him and help him with the money Adam has saved.

1 *memory* – "reminder" (Orlando was so like his father that the sight of him reminded Adam of Sir Rowland).

2 *make you* – "you are doing".

FIRST LORD

I cannot hear of any that did see her.
The ladies, her attendants² of her chamber,   5
Saw her a-bed, and in the morning early
They found the bed untreasured³ of their mistress.

SECOND LORD

My lord, the roynish⁴ clown, at whom so oft⁵
Your Grace was wont⁶ to laugh, is also missing.
Hisperia, the princess' gentlewoman,⁷   10
Confesses that she secretly o'erheard
Your daughter and her cousin much commend
The parts and graces⁸ of the wrestler
That did but lately foil⁹ the sinewy Charles;
And she believes, wherever they are gone,   15
That youth is surely in their company.

DUKE FREDERICK

Send to his brother, fetch that gallant¹⁰ hither;
If he be absent, bring his brother to me;
I 'll make him find him. Do this suddenly¹¹
And let not search and inquisition¹² quail   20
To bring again¹³ these foolish runaways.

[*Exeunt*

Scene III. Outside Oliver's house.
Enter ORLANDO *and* ADAM, *meeting.*

ORLANDO

Who 's there?

ADAM

What, my young master? O my gentle master!
O my sweet master! O you memory¹
Of old Sir Rowland! Why, what make you² here?

61

3 *virtuous* – "good in every way". Adam's question means: "You are a thoroughly good man, but for that very reason you are in danger".

4 *wherefore* – "for what reason" (the question has the same general meaning as the *Why* questions – see note 3 above).

5 *so fond . . . Duke* – "so foolish as to defeat the big prize-fighter *(bonny prizer)* of the angry Duke" (Charles was a *prizer*, or prize-fighter, because he earned his living by wrestling; *humorous* – "too easily made angry").

6 *to some kind . . . yours* (line 12) – "there are certain men whose own good qualities *(graces)* only do them harm? That is what *your* good qualities do to you".

7 *Your virtues . . . traitors to you:* Adam is still saying that Orlando's goodness is putting him in danger. In the metaphor here the virtues are compared to *traitors* trying to cause Orlando's death, yet with a saintly *(sanctified)* and holy appearance.

8 *is comely . . . bears it* – "looks beautiful *(is comely)* poisons *(Envenoms)* the person who wears it". As an example of something that is good doing harm. Shakespeare seems to be referring to the shirt of Nessus (see p. 30, note 111), but it was poisoned and caused him terrible pain and, in the end, death.

9 *within this . . . lives* – "the man who hates you for your good qualities *(graces)* lives in this house *(within this roof)*".

10 *I will not . . . son:* Adam feels that Oliver does not deserve to be called the son of Sir Rowland.

11 *lodging . . . within it* – "the building in which you always sleep, and burn you in the fire". We suppose from evidence in Act I Scene i that Orlando had to sleep in one of the farm buildings at some distance from the house. Such buildings were usually wooden ones in Shakespeare's time.

12 *cut you off* – "kill you".

13 *practices* – "plots".

14 *but a butchery* – "just a place of death (for you)" *(butchery,* a place where butchers kill animals, used metaphorically for a place of murder).

15 *wouldst . . . me go* – "do you wish me to go".

16 *No matter . . . here* – "It does not matter where (you go), provided that you do not come here".

Why are you virtuous?[3] Why do people love you?   5
And wherefore[4] are you gentle, strong, and valiant?
Why would you be so fond[5] to overcome
The bonny prizer of the humorous Duke?
Your praise is come too swiftly home before you.
Know you not, master, to some kind[6] of men   10
Their graces serve them but as enemies?
No more do yours. Your virtues, gentle master,
Are sanctified[7] and holy traitors to you.
O, what a world is this, when what is comely[8]
Envenoms him that bears it!   15

ORLANDO

Why, what 's the matter?

ADAM

                    O unhappy youth,
Come not within these doors; within this roof[9]
The enemy of all your graces lives.
Your brother – no, no brother, yet the son –
Yet not the son, I will not call him son[10]   20
Of him I was about to call his father –
Hath heard your praises, and this night he means
To burn the lodging where you use[11] to lie
And you within it. If he fail of that,
He will have other means to cut you off.[12]   25
I overheard him, and his practices;[13]
This is no place, this house is but a butchery;[14]
Abhor it, fear it, do not enter it!

ORLANDO

Why, whither, Adam, wouldst thou have[15] me go?

ADAM

No matter whither, so[16] you come not here.   30

63

17 *with a base . . . road* – "as a robber, make wrong and violent use of a sword to force people on the public roads to give me what I need in order to live". (A gentleman could not do this; it was a *base* – low and bad – use of a sword. Orlando has no training for any gentlemanly work, but he will not become one of the many highway robbers.)

18 *do how I can* – "whatever else I may have to do".

19 *subject me . . . brother* – "suffer the dangerous hatred of an unnatural and murderous brother" (*diverted blood*: the idea is that the course of nature, in which brothers love each other, has been turned aside, or *diverted*, in Oliver).

20 *do not so* – "do not do that" (i.e. risk Oliver's hatred).

21 *thrifty hire I saved* – "wages (*hire*) I saved with care" (*thrifty* – "careful with money"). Adam must have been well paid by Sir Rowland and very thrifty: a *crown* was a gold coin worth 25p and of much greater purchasing power than that amount today.

22 *did store . . . thrown* (line 42) – "was saving to provide for me (*be my foster-nurse* – literally, "be the woman who is not a baby's mother but who feeds it") when the strength to work as a servant has left my old limbs and I am treated as useless and unwanted" (the image in line 42 is of age as a worn-out instrument thrown aside).

23 *that*, i.e. the 500 crowns.

24 *He that . . . feed*, i.e. God. (The *raven* is a large black bird of the crow family. The reference is to the Bible, *Job* 38:41 "who provideth for the raven its food".)

25 *Yea . . . sparrow* – "yes, (and) with special care for each one of them (*providently*), supplies food (*caters*) for the sparrows (the commonest birds of all)" (Bible, *Luke* 12:6: "not one (sparrow) of them is forgotten by God").

26 *lusty* – "vigorous". (This is also the meaning in line 52.)

27 *did apply . . . debility* (line 51) – "put into my blood strong drinks (*liquors*) which heat it and are harmful (*rebellious*) to health, or (*Nor*) go shamelessly (*with unbashful forehead*) to seek (*woo*) those things which cause weakness and illness".

28 *frosty, but kindly*, i.e. with white hair – like the frozen dew (*frost*) of a cold winter's day – but natural and pleasant (*kindly*).

29 *business* – "affairs".

30 *how well . . . world* – "what a good example you are of the faithful (*constant*) service given in the old times".

31 *service sweat . . . meed* – "servants worked hard (*sweat*, for *sweated*) because it was their duty, and not just for reward (*meed*)".

32 *art not . . . fashion* – "do not follow the ways".

33 *having that . . . the having* – "when once they have that (i.e. promotion to a higher rank), they stop giving any service because they no longer need to serve"; *choke*, literally, "block".

ORLANDO

What, wouldst thou have me go and beg my food?
Or with a base[17] and boisterous sword enforce
A thievish living on the common road?
This I must do, or know not what to do;
Yet this I will not do, do how I can.[18]   35
I rather will subject[19] me to the malice
Of a diverted blood and bloody brother.

ADAM

But do not so.[20] I have five hundred crowns,
The thrifty hire[21] I saved under your father,
Which I did store[22] to be my foster-nurse   40
When service should in my old limbs lie lame,
And unregarded age in corners thrown.
Take that[23] and He that doth the ravens[24] feed,
Yea, providently caters[25] for the sparrow,
Be comfort to my age. Here is the gold;   45
All this I give you. Let me be your servant;
Though I look old, yet I am strong and lusty;[26]
For in my youth I never did apply
Hot and rebellious liquors[27] in my blood,
Nor did not with unbashful forehead woo   50
The means of weakness and debility;
Therefore my age is as a lusty winter,
Frosty,[28] but kindly. Let me go with you;
I'll do the service of a younger man
In all your business[29] and necessities.   55

ORLANDO

O good old man, how well in thee appears[30]
The constant service of the antique world;
When service sweat[31] for duty, not for meed!
Thou art not for the fashion[32] of these times,
Where none will sweat but for promotion,   60
And having that,[33] do choke their service up

34 *thou prun'st . . . husbandry* (line 65), i.e. trying to help someone who will never be able to pay you back. The literal meaning is: "you are carefully cutting back the branches of *(prun'st)* a tree which is unhealthy *(rotten)* and so cannot produce even a flower *(blossom)* in return for *(In lieu of)* all your trouble and skilful care *(pains and husbandry)*". A good tree is pruned to make it produce more and better fruit.

35 *come thy ways* – "come along".

36 *youthful wages* – "wages earned when you were young".

37 *light upon . . . content* – "find some settled and contented, even if humble *(low)*, way of living". Orlando's last two lines rhyme, and the whole of Adam's following speech is in lines which rhyme in pairs (couplets). The effect is to suggest to the audience that the scene is coming to an end, and to fix attention on Adam's words, which express the spirit of true faithfulness.

38 *till . . . fourscore* – "until now, when I am nearly eighty years old". (In line 74 *fourscore*, 4 × 20, also means eighty years old.)

39 *too late a week*, a saying which, like the modern "too late in the day", just means too late for a particular action, here for going to seek a new way of living.

40 *not . . . debtor* – "not owing anything to my master". Adam believes that he "owes" loyalty to the man he regards as the true son of Sir Rowland de Boys.

(II.iv) Rosalind, Celia, and Touchstone arrive in Arden, Rosalind disguised as a boy. They hear Silvius, a young shepherd, talking to the old shepherd Corin about his unhappy love. Later they speak to Corin, and arrange for him to buy with their money a cottage and its grounds on the edge of the forest.

1 *disgrace my man's apparel*, i.e. shame (by crying) my appearance of being a man *(apparel*-clothes).

2 *weaker vessel*, a Bible description (I *Peter* 3:7) of a woman as less strong than a man.

3 *doublet . . . petticoat*, i.e. a man must show himself brave in the presence of a woman. Rosalind is wearing a man's clothes – *doublet*, a short, close-fitting coat, and *hose*, a long tight garment for the legs. Celia is dressed as a girl, in a *petticoat*.

Even with the having; it is not so with thee.
But, poor old man, thou prun'st a rotten tree[34]
That cannot so much as a blossom yield
In lieu of all thy pains and husbandry.   65
But come thy ways,[35] we 'll go along together,
And ere we have thy youthful[36] wages spent,
We 'll light upon[37] some settled low content.

ADAM

Master, go on, and I will follow thee
To the last gasp, with truth and loyalty.   70
From seventeen years till now almost fourscore[38]
Here livéd I, but now live here no more.
At seventeen years many their fortunes seek,
But at fourscore it is too late a week;[39]
Yet fortune cannot recompense me better   75
Than to die well, and not my master's debtor.[40]

[*Exeunt*

Scene IV. The Forest of Arden.

Enter ROSALIND *disguised as* GANYMEDE, CELIA *as*
ALIENA, *and* TOUCHSTONE.

ROSALIND

O Jupiter, how weary are my spirits!

TOUCHSTONE

I care not for my spirits, if my legs were not weary.

ROSALIND

I could find in my heart to disgrace my man's apparel[1] and to
cry like a woman; but I must comfort the weaker vessel,[2] as
doublet and hose[3] ought to show itself courageous to petticoat: 5
therefore, courage, good Aliena.

67

4 *bear* – "be patient".

5 *For my part . . . bear you* – "I myself would rather be patient with *(bear with)* you than carry *(bear)* you". Touchstone continues to play on the two uses of *bear* in what follows.

6 *bear no cross* has two meanings, and Touchstone plays with them: (i) "not suffer" – the saying "bear a cross" referred to a part of the Roman punishment suffered by Christ – (ii) "not carry any money" – because a *cross* was a coin.

7 *the more fool I* – "which makes me even more of a fool".

8 *that* – "I wish that".

9 *upon a . . . pillow* – "when he was in bed (with his head on a pillow) at midnight".

10 *As sure . . . love so* – "although I really think that no man was ever so deeply in love before".

11 *drawn to . . . fantasy* – "led into doing by your imagination (under the influence of love)".

doublet and hose[3]

CELIA

I pray you, bear[4] with me; I cannot go no further.

TOUCHSTONE

For my part,[5] I had rather bear with you than bear you; yet I
should bear no cross[6] if I did bear you; for I think you have no
money in your purse.   10

ROSALIND

Well, this is the Forest of Arden.

TOUCHSTONE

Ay, now am I in Arden; the more fool I;[7] when I was at home,
I was in a better place; but travellers must be content.

Enter CORIN *and* SILVIUS

ROSALIND

Ay, be so, good Touchstone. Look you, who comes here; a
young man and an old in solemn talk.   [*They stand back*   15

CORIN

That is the way to make her scorn you still.

SILVIUS

O Corin, that[8] thou knew'st how I do love her!

CORIN

I partly guess, for I have loved ere now.

SILVIUS

No, Corin, being old, thou canst not guess,
Though in thy youth thou wast as true a lover   20
As ever sighed upon a midnight pillow.[9]
But if thy love were ever like to mine –
As sure I think[10] did never man love so –
How many actions most ridiculous
Hast thou been drawn to by thy fantasy?[11]   25

69

12 *heartily* – "deeply and sincerely".

13 *run into* – "enter into without thought". (Because Corin, an old man, has forgotten the foolish things he did as a young lover, Silvius is sure that Corin can never have been so deeply in love as he is himself.)

14 *Wearing . . . praise* – "wearying the person you are speaking to by (endless) praise of the woman whom you love".

15 *Searching . . . mine own*, i.e. hearing the expression of Silvius's suffering has made Rosalind realise that she herself is suffering from love. – Her metaphor gives us an image of a doctor opening up *(Searching)* a wound and as a painful discovery *(by hard adventure)* finding the cause.

16 *bid him take that* – "told him to have my sword-cut as a punishment".

17 *batler*, a stick with a flat end, used for beating clothes while washing them. (Touchstone's account of his follies as a lover makes fun of the excesses of romantic love – see Introduction, p. xv.)

18 *chopt*, (modern *chapped*) with the skin made rough and broken by cold weather.

19 *peascod*, the green soft shell in which peas grow.

20 *cods* – "peas".

21 *again* – "back" (Jane Smile was removing the peas from their shells at the time).

22 *mortal in folly* – "likely to do all sorts of foolish things". Touchstone is playing with two meanings of *mortal*: (i) "not living for ever" *(all is mortal in nature)*, and (ii) "extreme" *(mortal in folly*, extremely foolish).

23 *thou art ware of* – "you realise" *(ware* for *aware*, knowing).

24 *be ware . . . it*: i.e. never learn to beware of my own cleverness until it hurts me. (Touchstone uses a different *ware*, meaning "careful").

70

CORIN

Into a thousand that I have forgotten.

SILVIUS

O, thou didst then ne'er love so heartily![12]
If thou remember'st not the slightest folly
That ever love did make thee run into,[13]
Thou hast not loved.   30
Or if thou hast not sat as I do now,
Wearing[14] thy hearer in thy mistress' praise,
Thou hast not loved.
Or if thou hast not broke from company
Abruptly, as my passion now makes me,   35
Thou has not loved.
O Phebe, Phebe, Phebe!   [*Exit*

ROSALIND

Alas, poor shepherd! Searching of[15] thy wound,
I have by hard adventure found mine own.

TOUCHSTONE

And I mine. I remember, when I was in love, I broke my sword   40
upon a stone and bid him take that[16] for coming a-night to Jane
Smile: and I remember the kissing of her batler,[17] and the cow's
dugs that her pretty chopt[18] hands had milked; and I remember
the wooing of a peascod[19] instead of her; from whom I took
two cods,[20] and giving her them again,[21] said with weeping   45
tears: "Wear these for my sake." We that are true lovers run
into strange capers; but as all is mortal in nature, so is all nature
in love mortal[22] in folly.

ROSALIND

Thou speakest wiser than thou art ware[23] of.

TOUCHSTONE

Nay, I shall ne'er be ware[24] of mine own wit till I break my   50
shins against it.

71

25 *upon my fashion* – "like my own".
26 *it grows . . . with me* – "it is getting rather old *(stale)* in my case".
27 *gold* – "money".
28 *Holla, you clown* – "Listen, you country fellow". Touchstone shouts to Corin from a distance. He is glad that Celia has given him the chance to behave like a courtier ready to offer money to the humble country fellow *(clown* – but, as Rosalind quickly points out, *clown* also means a fool like himself).

29 *Peace* – "Be quiet".
30 *thy kinsman* – "related to you" (as a *clown*).
31 *Your betters* – "People of a higher rank in society than yourself".
32 *Else are they* – "If they are not (better than myself), they are" (*Else* – "Otherwise").
33 *even* – "evening".

ROSALIND

I prithee, shepherd, if that[34] love or gold   65
Can in this desert[35] place buy entertainment,[36]
Bring us where we may rest ourselves and feed.
Here 's a young maid with travel much oppressed,[37]
And faints for succour.

CORIN

            Fair sir, I pity her,
And wish, for her sake more than for mine own,   70
My fortunes were more able[38] to relieve her;
But I am shepherd to another man,
And do not shear the fleeces that I graze.[39]
My master is of churlish[40] disposition,
And little recks[41] to find the way to heaven   75
By doing deeds of hospitality.
Besides, his cote,[42] his flocks, and bounds of feed[43]
Are now on sale, and at our sheepcote[44] now,
By reason[45] of his absence, there is nothing
That you will feed on;[46] but what is, come see,   80
And in my voice[47] most welcome shall you be.

ROSALIND

What[48] is he that shall buy his flock and pasture?

CORIN

That young swain[49] that you saw here but erewhile,[50]
That little cares[51] for buying anything.

ROSALIND

I pray thee, if it stand[52] with honesty,   85
Buy thou the cottage, pasture, and the flock,
And thou shalt have[53] to pay for it of us.

CELIA

And we will mend[54] thy wages. I like this place
And willingly could waste[55] my time in it.

56 *Assuredly* – "Certainly". Corin is answering Rosalind's doubt about whether the purchase could be made "with *honesty*" (note 52, p. 74).

57 *upon report* – "after getting a (full) description".

58 *feeder* – "servant" (depending on his master for food).

59 *right suddenly* – "at once".

(II.v) Duke Senior's companions sing *Under the greenwood tree*, expressing the pleasures of a simple life. Jaques talks to them and adds to the song a mocking verse of his own.

1 *greenwood tree* – "tree in the forest". The word *greenwood* often meant the place where men like Robin Hood (see I.i.95) lived in hiding.

2 *Who loves to lie* – "Anyone who likes to live".

3 *turn . . . throat* – "compose a cheerful tune like the sweet song of a bird". (A *turn* was a musical composition; *throat*, from which the song comes, is used for the song itself.)

4 *thank it* – "am glad of it".

5 *as a weasel sucks eggs:* The weasel, a small four-footed animal, sucks out the liquid contained in birds' eggs. The image is of melancholy destroying life: it warns us against approving too completely of Jaques's character.

6 *ragged* – "rough".

CORIN

Assuredly[56] the thing is to be sold.   90
Go with me; if you like upon report[57]
The soil, the profit, and this kind of life,
I will your very faithful feeder[58] be
And buy it with your gold right suddenly.[59]

[*Exeunt*

Scene V. The forest.

Enter AMIENS, JAQUES, *and others.*

AMIENS [*Singing*]
Under the greenwood[1] tree
Who[2] loves to lie with me,
And turn[3] his merry note
Unto the sweet bird's throat,
Come hither, come hither, come hither: 5
Here shall he see
No enemy
But winter and rough weather.

JAQUES

More, more, I prithee more.

AMIENS

It will make you melancholy, Monsieur Jaques.   10

JAQUES

I thank[4] it. More, I prithee, more. I can suck melancholy out of
a song as a weasel sucks eggs.[5] More, I prithee, more.

AMIENS

My voice is ragged:[6] I know I cannot please you.

77

7 *stanzo*, for *stanza* – "verse of a song". The word, borrowed from Italian, was new in English at the time of this play.

8 *What you will* – "You can call them stanzos or stanzas or anything you like".

9 *they owe me nothing*: Jaques says jokingly that he is interested in names only if they are the names of people who owe him money. He is not interested in the name "stanza".

10 *that they call . . . beggarly thanks* (line 23), i.e. "the polite behaviour of gentlemen towards each other is like a meeting between two monkeys; when a man gives me warm thanks, I feel as if I have paid him some money and he thanks me for it as beggars do" (*dog-apes*, baboons, monkeys with dog-like faces, which were dangerous although they looked friendly; *renders* – "gives back". Jaques does not thank people because such politeness is so seldom sincere.

11 *hold your tongues* – "be silent".

12 *cover the while* – "lay the table while I am singing".

13 *to look you* – "looking for you".

14 *disputable* – "fond of argument".

15 *warble* – "sing as a bird does, varying the tune" (as in the "Come hither" line of the song that follows).

16 *i' the sun* – "in the sunshine".

JAQUES

I do not desire you to please me; I do desire you to sing. Come, more; another stanzo.[7] Call you 'em stanzos? 15

AMIENS

What you will,[8] Monsieur Jaques.

JAQUES

Nay, I care not for their names; they owe[9] me nothing. Will you sing?

AMIENS

More at your request than to please myself.

JAQUES

Well then, if ever I thank any man, I 'll thank you. But that they 20
call compliment[10] is like th' encounter of two dog-apes, and
when a man thanks me heartily, methinks I have given him a
penny, and he renders me the beggarly thanks. Come, sing; and
you that will not, hold your tongues.[11]

AMIENS

Well, I 'll end the song. Sirs, cover the while;[12] the Duke will 25
drink under this tree. [*To* JAQUES] He hath been all this day
to look[13] you.

JAQUES

And I have been all this day to avoid him. He is too disputable[14]
for my company: I think of as many matters as he, but I give
heaven thanks and make no boast of them. Come, warble,[15] 30
come.

Song

All together

Who doth ambition shun
And loves to live i' the sun,[16]

79

17 *note* – "tune".

18 *in despite of my invention* – "(just) to punish my imagination" (for trying to write poetry: Jaques thinks poets are foolish).

19 *come to pass* – "happen".

20 *turn ass* – "become a fool" (*ass* – "donkey").

21 *a stubborn . . . please* – "to please his (or someone else's) stubborn desires"; *stubborn*, determined to do as one wishes, without listening to argument.

22 *Ducdame* (pronounced with three sounded vowels): The word seems to have no meaning, and is only sung to go with the tune. Jaques's explanation in line 53 is joking, we suppose (although the word *may* have been "magic"), but the others gather round as they sing, and Jaques makes this his opportunity to call them fools.

23 *Gross* – "as big".

24 *An if* – "if".

25 *to call . . . circle*, i.e. to draw fools by this magic word into a charmed circle, from which they cannot get away (compare v.iv. 34).

26 *the first-born of Egypt*: According to the Bible (*Exodus* 11), God destroyed the eldest son *(first-born)* of every Egyptian family including that of the ruler. Perhaps Jaques means that he will speak out against everyone he dislikes.

27 *banquet* – "light meal".

<blockquote>
Seeking the food he eats,
And pleased with what he gets,   35
Come hither, come hither, come hither.
Here shall he see
No enemy
But winter and rough weather.
</blockquote>

JAQUES

I 'll give you a verse to this note[17] that I made yesterday, in   40
despite[18] of my invention.

AMIENS

And I 'll sing it.

JAQUES

Thus it goes:

<blockquote>
If it do come to pass[19]
That any man turn ass,[20]   45
Leaving his wealth and ease
A stubborn will to please,[21]
Ducdame,[22] ducdame, ducdame:
Here shall he see
Gross[23] fools as he,   50
An if[24] he will come to me.
</blockquote>

AMIENS

What 's that "ducdame"?

JAQUES

'T is a Greek invocation, to call fools into a circle.[25] I 'll go
sleep, if I can; if I cannot, I 'll rail against all the first-born[26] of
Egypt.   55

AMIENS

And I 'll go seek the Duke: his banquet[27] is prepared.

[*Exeunt in different directions*

81

(II.vi) Orlando and Adam arrive in the forest. Exposed to the hard conditions of nature, Adam is dying of hunger. Orlando leaves him in order to go in search of food.

1 *die for food* – "am dying for want of food".

2 *measure out my grave* – "mark out (by lying down) the length of my grave".

3 *how now* – "what is the matter".

4 *heart* – "courage".

5 *Live . . . comfort* – "Keep living for a little while longer; take comfort".

6 *If this uncouth . . . to thee* – "If there is a wild animal of any kind *(anything savage)* in this strange *(uncouth)* forest, I will either be killed and eaten by it or kill it and bring it to you for a meal".

7 *Thy conceit . . . powers* – "You are nearer to death in your imagination *(conceit)* than in reality *(powers*, bodily strength)".

8 *be comfortable* – "stay cheerful".

9 *at the arm's end* – "at a distance" (modern "at arm's length").

10 *presently* – "very soon".

11 *leave* – "permission".

12 *a mocker of my labour*, i.e. making me waste my efforts *(mocker* – "one who disappoints").

13 *Well said . . . cheerly* – "Good! You look more cheerful" (Adam has given a faint smile, and Orlando encourages him).

14 *Cheerly* – "Cheer up".

(II.vii) Jaques tells Duke Senior how he met Touchstone in the forest; he describes Touchstone as a wise fool, and speaks of the opportunities so-called fools have of expressing their true thoughts about the evils of society. Orlando appears on the scene, threatening to use force if food is not supplied for Adam and himself. The Duke, with his natural kindness, makes Orlando welcome, and he goes to fetch Adam. Jaques meanwhile expresses some thoughts about life and speaks of how "All the world's a stage". Adam is brought in, and while Orlando tells his story to the Duke, Amiens sings the song "Blow, blow, thou winter wind", telling of how man's ingratitude is harder to bear than nature's cruelty.

1 *like* – "in the shape of".

2 *but even now* – "only just".

Scene VI. The forest.

Enter ORLANDO, supporting ADAM.

ADAM

Dear master, I can go no further. O, I die[1] for food. Here lie I
down and measure[2] out my grave. Farewell, kind master.

ORLANDO

Why, how now,[3] Adam? No greater heart[4] in thee? Live a
little, comfort[5] a little, cheer thyself a little. If this uncouth[6]
forest yield anything savage, I will either be food for it or   5
bring it for food to thee. Thy conceit[7] is nearer death than
thy powers. For my sake be comfortable;[8] hold death awhile
at the arm's end.[9] I will here be with thee presently,[10] and if
I bring thee not something to eat, I will give thee leave[11] to
die: but if thou diest before I come, thou art a mocker[12] of   10
my labour. Well said! Thou lookest cheerly,[13] and I 'll be with
thee quickly. Yet thou liest in the bleak air: come, I will
bear thee to some shelter, and thou shalt not die for lack of a
dinner, if there live anything in this desert. Cheerly,[14] good
Adam!   15

[*Exeunt*

Scene VII. The forest.

A table laid for a meal. Enter DUKE SENIOR, AMIENS, and Lords, dressed like outlaws.

DUKE SENIOR

I think he be transformed into a beast,
For I can nowhere find him like[1] a man.

FIRST LORD

My lord, he is but even[2] now gone hence:
Here was he merry, hearing of a song.

83

3 *If he, compact . . . spheres: Discord* is the opposite of *harmony*. Duke Senior reflects the belief that the stars moved round the earth in *spheres*, which turned with a smooth, harmonious motion, making music in heaven. Men whose character was agreeable and harmonious loved music because it was made up of the same qualities. But Jaques's character was made up *(compact)* of discords *(jars)* – qualities which did not agree with one another. It was as hard to imagine him as a music lover as to imagine discord in heaven.

4 *my labour* – "me the trouble (of seeking him)".

5 *what a life* – "what a strange state of affairs".

6 *woo* – "seek for".

7 *What . . . merrily* – "You look surprisingly cheerful".

8 *motley* – "wearing *motley* (the special patched coat of many colours worn by court 'fools')". Jaques refers to Touchstone, a professional "fool".

9 *A miserable world:* Even when he is amused, Jaques does not forget to give expression to his usual melancholy.

10 *As* – "As true as".

11 *Lady Fortune:* See p. 14, note 20, and Introduction, p. xix.

12 *set terms,* i.e. forms of speech such as were listed *(set)* by teachers of the art of public speaking.

13 *morrow* – "morning".

14 *Call me . . . fortune,* i.e. only good fortune would make him really a fool. Just as Duke Senior believes that misfortune brings benefits (II.i.12), Touchstone believes that good fortune makes men foolish.

15 *a dial . . . poke* – "a watch from his pocket". (Pocket watches were not common in Shakespeare's time, but they were made in England from about 1540. They had one hand, which showed the hours.)

16 *wags* – "runs on".

17 *but an hour ago* – "only an hour".

18 *ripe and ripe* – "grow riper and riper" (like fruit on a tree).

19 *rot,* i.e. become old and useless (again like fruit if it is left on the tree).

20 *thereby . . . tale* – "there is a moral lesson to be learnt from that".

21 *moral . . . time* – "find a moral in connection with (a simple matter like telling the) time".

22 *My lungs . . . chanticleer* – "I began to laugh as loudly as a cock *(chanticleer)* crows".

A motley⁸ fool

DUKE SENIOR

If he, compact of jars,[3] grow musical,   5
We shall have shortly discord in the spheres.
Go seek him; tell him I would speak with him.

Enter JAQUES

FIRST LORD

He saves my labour[4] by his own approach.

DUKE SENIOR

Why, how now, monsieur! What a life[5] is this,
That your poor friends must woo[6] your company?   10
What,[7] you look merrily.

JAQUES

A fool, a fool! I met a fool i' th' forest,
A motley[8] fool! A miserable world![9]
As[10] I do live by food, I met a fool;
Who laid him down and basked him in the sun   15
And railed on Lady Fortune[11] in good terms,
In good set terms,[12] and yet a motley fool.
"Good morrow,[13] fool," quoth I. "No, sir," quoth he,
"Call me not fool till heaven hath sent me fortune."[14]
And then he drew a dial[15] from his poke,   20
And looking on it with lacklustre eye,
Says very wisely, "It is ten o'clock:
Thus we may see," quoth he, "how the world wags:[16]
'T is but an hour ago[17] since it was nine,
And after one hour more 't will be eleven;   25
And so, from hour to hour, we ripe[18] and ripe,
And then, from hour to hour, we rot[19] and rot;
And thereby[20] hangs a tale." When I did hear
The motley fool thus moral[21] on the time,
My lungs began to crow[22] like chanticleer   30
That fools should be so deep contemplative;

85

23 *sans intermission* – "without a pause". *sans*: "without" (French).

24 *Motley's . . . wear* – "Motley is the only proper dress", i.e. fools are the only sensible people.

25 *if ladies . . . know it* – "if ladies are nothing more than young and beautiful, they have at least the advantage of knowing that they are". (They may seem to have no brains but they have the one piece of knowledge that they need – the knowledge of their own beauty.)

26 *as dry . . . mangled forms* (line 42) – "as dried up as sailors' food at the end of a voyage, he has a great store of information and observation, which he gives out *(vents)* in a confused mixture". Sea voyages in the sixteenth century often lasted for many months. The sailors' food, baked in hard flat cakes *(biscuit)* in order to preserve it, was extremely dry and hard by the end of the voyage, if there was any left *(remainder)*. Jaques uses this image because it was believed that good memory was a quality found in dry brains.

27 *I am ambitious . . . coat*, i.e. he would like to wear the clothes – and have the privileges – of a fool. In the next line Duke Senior jokingly promises to make Jaques his court fool. Jaques declares (lines 44–51) that he would indeed like that; then he would have freedom to criticise everyone – a privilege no ruler would grant to those who were thought wise.

28 *suit* – (i) "request", and (ii) "clothing" (Jaques means the first, with word-play on the second).

29 *weed . . . am wise* – "remove from your mind any unwanted idea that I am wise". (The image is of having to get rid of weeds which grow thick and coarse *(rank)* where they are not wanted.)

30 *Withal* – "with this (position of court fool)".

31 *as large . . . please* – "as full a right *(charter)* to speak against anyone I wish *(please)* as the wind has to blow on anyone".

32 *so* – "this (right) is what".

33 *galled with my folly* – "hurt by the thoughts I speak as a court fool". If a wise man is mocked by a court fool, he will laugh at the joke; a look of annoyance would let everyone know that he takes the fool's criticism seriously. Even when the fool's jokes are not directed against him, they will be seen to hurt him unless he joins in the laugh (lines 51–7).

34 *The why . . . church* – "The reason is as easy to find as the local church". (Everybody who lives in the *parish*, or district served by a church, knows the way to the church. Probably there is a play on *why* and *way*, which were nearer in sound than they are now.)

35 *He that . . . bob* – "the man who receives a fool's wise criticism is acting *(Doth)* very foolishly if he does not pretend not to notice the attack, although he may feel the pain *(smart)*".

36 *if not . . . glances of the fool* – "otherwise even the unaimed hits *(squandering glances)* of the fool will show up in detail the wise man's weaknesses". (The fool attacks a certain weakness without knowing that it is Lord A's or Lord B's weakness. If Lord A or Lord B does not laugh at the joke, the other people present will understand that the fool is speaking of him, and his secret weakness will be known.)

37 *Invest* – "Dress" (as for a ceremony).

And I did laugh sans intermission,[23]
An hour by his dial. O noble fool!
A worthy fool! Motley's the only wear.[24]

DUKE SENIOR

What fool is this?   35

JAQUES

O worthy fool! One that hath been a courtier,
And says, if ladies be but young and fair,[25]
They have the gift to know it; and in his brain,
Which is as dry[26] as the remainder biscuit
After a voyage, he hath strange places crammed   40
With observation, the which he vents
In mangled forms. O that I were a fool!
I am ambitious[27] for a motley coat.

DUKE SENIOR

Thou shalt have one.

JAQUES

                    It is my only suit,[28]
Provided that you weed[29] your better judgments   45
Of all opinion that grows rank in them
That I am wise. I must have liberty
Withal,[30] as large a charter[31] as the wind,
To blow on whom I please; for so[32] fools have,
And they that are most gallèd[33] with my folly,   50
They most must laugh. And why, sir, must they so?
The why[34] is plain as way to parish church:
He that a fool doth very wisely hit[35]
Doth very foolishly, although he smart,
Not to seem senseless of the bob; if not,   55
The wise man's folly is anatomised[36]
Even by the squandering glances of the fool.
Invest[37] me in my motley, give me leave
To speak my mind, and I will through and through

38 *Cleanse . . . world:* The image is of the world (i.e. society) as a body which is diseased *(foul* and *infected)* and needs to be made pure again by a doctor.

39 *medicine,* i.e. criticism.

40 *Fie on thee* – "You should be ashamed of yourself".

41 *for a counter,* i.e. as a small bet (a promise that a *counter* – a small, almost worthless coin – would be paid if the answer given was not right).

42 *Most mischievous . . . chiding sin* – "(You intend to do) very harmful wickedness *(sin)* by blaming other people for their wickedness". The Duke says (lines 64-9) that Jaques is himself a sinner and wants to put the blame for his own faults and vices on the rest of society.

43 *brutish sting* – "animal-like *(brutish)* urge *(sting)* of desire".

44 *all the embossed . . . general world* – "you want to pour out *(disgorge)* on to the other people in the world all the swollen *(embossed)* sores and diseases at their worst *(headed)* that you have given to yourself by being free to live without any control *(with license of free foot)*". Jaques should not wish to blame others for his own faults, which he has caught like diseases because of his free, wandering life. In reply (lines 70-87) Jaques declares that he does not want to attack particular individuals but types and classes of people. If any one person complains, that proves that the criticism applies to him. (This was the usual argument of writers and critics of Shakespeare's time when they were blamed for insulting other people in their poems and plays.)

45 *who cries . . . party,* i.e. if someone complains about *(cries out on)* proud behaviour he cannot be said to blame *(tax)* any particular person *(private party).*

46 *Doth it . . . sea,* i.e. pride spreads in all directions like a great sea. The image of the sea is continued in the *vb* ("retreat like the tide") of the next line, which probably means that there is no end to the display which pride demands except the exhaustion of the wealth that supports it.

47 *When that* – "if".

48 *the city woman . . . princes* – "a citizen's wife wears clothes so costly that only rulers *(princes)* could afford to pay for them".

49 *on unworthy shoulders,* i.e. her back is not so beautiful as to be fit for such fine clothes.

50 *come in* – "be offended".

51 *such a one . . . neighbour* – "her neighbour is (in this matter of dressing too expensively) exactly like herself".

52 *what is he . . . speech* (line 82) – "if a man in the lowest position in society *(of basest function)* thinks that I am attacking him personally, and therefore says that (it is not my business how he dresses because) I do not have to pay for all his fine clothes *(bravery),* he is by that defence *(therein)* showing that it is his own folly that I have named in my speech".

53 *There . . . What then* – "There is my opinion. What can you say against it?"

54 *wherein my tongue* – "in what way my words" *wronged:* "harmed".

55 *if it do him right,* i.e. if the description fits his character.

56 *if he be free . . . of any man* – "if he has *not* got the folly I have attacked, then my attack *(taxing)* flies away without applying to anyone – like the wild goose flying past and not owned *(Unclaimed)* by anyone".

Cleanse the foul body[38] of the infected world,   60
If they will patiently receive my medicine.[39]

DUKE SENIOR

Fie on thee![40] I can tell what thou wouldst do.

JAQUES

What, for a counter,[41] would I do but good?

DUKE SENIOR

Most mischievous[42] foul sin, in chiding sin;
For thou thyself hast been a libertine,   65
As sensual as the brutish sting[43] itself;
And all the embosséd[44] sores and headed evils
That thou with license of free foot hast caught,
Wouldst thou disgorge into the general world.

JAQUES

Why, who cries out[45] on pride,   70
That can therein tax any private party?
Doth it not flow as hugely[46] as the sea,
Till that the weary very means do ebb?
What woman in the city do I name,
When that[47] I say the city woman bears   75
The cost[48] of princes on unworthy shoulders?[49]
Who can come in[50] and say that I mean her,
When such a one as she,[51] such is her neighbour?
Or, what is he[52] of basest function
That says his bravery is not on my cost,   80
Thinking that I mean him, but therein suits
His folly to the mettle of my speech?
There then![53] How then? What then? Let me see wherein
My tongue[54] hath wronged him: if it do him right,[55]
Then he hath wronged himself: if he be free,[56]   85
Why, then my taxing like a wild goose flies
Unclaimed of any man. But who comes here?

57 *Forbear* – "Stand back".

58 *eat none* – "eaten nothing".

59 *necessity*, i.e. those in real need.

60 *Of what . . . come of* – "What sort of rude fellow is this". (Literally, "What kind of cock is he?" *Cock* was used to describe a noisy person.)

61 *boldened* – "made bold and rough".

62 *Or else . . . empty* – "Or are you rather a violent *(rude)* man, a scorner *(despiser)* of good manners, that you seem so lacking in politeness *(civility)*".

63 *touched . . . at first* – "were nearest the truth in your first question" (about distress). To *touch the vein* was an image from the practice of doctors, who used to find the blood-vessel *(vein)* for letting blood out as a treatment for illness.

64 *the thorny . . . civility* (line 96) – "real distress, like the sharp pain of being pierced by a thorn, has taken from me the appearance of smooth politeness".

65 *inland bred* – "brought up in a district near the capital", i.e. where manners are good, not as in the wilder parts of the country.

66 *know some nurture* – "have had some training".

67 *answered* – "attended to".

68 *I must die*: Orlando has threatened death to anyone who touches the food, his threat ending with the word *answered*. Jaques plays on this word when he says that if Orlando will not listen to reasonable talk, he (Jaques) will be forced to die of hunger.

69 *Your gentleness . . . gentleness* – "Gentle behaviour (by you) will more easily compel *(shall force)* us to help you than threats of force will cause us to be gentle".

Enter ORLANDO *with his sword drawn*

ORLANDO

Forbear,[57] and eat no more!

JAQUES

Why, I have eat none[58] yet.

ORLANDO

Nor shalt not, till necessity[59] be served.

JAQUES

Of what kind[60] should this cock come of?   90

DUKE SENIOR

Art thou thus boldened,[61] man, by thy distress?
Or else a rude despiser[62] of good manners,
That in civility thou seem'st so empty?

ORLANDO

You touched my vein[63] at first: the thorny point[64]
Of bare distress hath ta'en from me the show   95
Of smooth civility; yet am I inland bred[65]
And know some nurture.[66] But forbear, I say:
He dies that touches any of this fruit
Till I and my affairs are answeréd.[67]

JAQUES

An you will not be answered with reason, I must die.[68]   100

DUKE SENIOR

What would you have? Your gentleness shall force[69]
More than your force move us to gentleness.

ORLANDO

I almost die for food, and let me have it.

91

70 *here*, i.e. in the forest.

71 *countenance . . . commandment* – "appearance of a man who will force others to obey".

72 *Lose and neglect . . . time* – "allow the hours to creep by (i.e. let time pass) without making any use of them".

73 *knolled* – "sounded (to call people)". The more common form of the word is "knelled".

74 *enforcement* – "form of persuasion". Orlando takes the advice given by Duke Senior in lines 101–2.

75 *hide* – "put back into its case".

76 *engendered* – "brought into being".

77 *upon command . . . ministered* – "just as it pleases you whatever we have to offer in order to satisfy your need".

78 *Whiles* – "while".

79 *like a doe . . . fawn* – "I go (to find the one who depends on me) like a mother deer *(doe)* going to find its young one *(fawn)*".

80 *sufficed* – "given enough (to eat)".

81 *Oppressed . . . evils* – "(who is) weighed down with two severe causes of weakness".

DUKE SENIOR

Sit down and feed, and welcome to our table.

ORLANDO

Speak you so gently? Pardon me, I pray you.   105
I thought that all things had been savage here,[70]
And therefore put I on the countenance[71]
Of stern commandment. But whate'er you are
That in this desert inaccessible,
Under the shade of melancholy boughs,   110
Lose and neglect[72] the creeping hours of time;
If ever you have looked on better days,
If ever been where bells have knolled[73] to church,
If ever sat at any good man's feast,
If ever from your eyelids wiped a tear,   115
And know what 't is to pity and be pitied,
Let gentleness my strong enforcement[74] be;
In the which hope I blush, and hide[75] my sword.

DUKE SENIOR

True is it that we have seen better days,
And have with holy bell been knolled to church,   120
And sat at good men's feasts, and wiped our eyes
Of drops that sacred pity hath engendered;[76]
And therefore sit you down in gentleness,
And take upon command[77] what help we have
That to your wanting may be ministered.   125

ORLANDO

Then but forbear your food a little while,
Whiles,[78] like a doe,[79] I go to find my fawn
And give it food. There is an old poor man,
Who after me hath many a weary step
Limped in pure love. Till he first sufficed,[80]   130
Oppressed with[81] two weak evils, age and hunger,
I will not touch a bit.

82 *will nothing waste* – "will eat nothing".

83 *all alone* – "the only people who are".

84 *and universal theatre* – "theatre of all the world". The image is of life: all men act out their lives like characters in a play.

85 *presents . . . play in* – "has sadder scenes *(pageants)* to show than the one in which we ourselves are playing parts". This prepares for Jaques's long and famous·description (lines 138–65) of the seven ages of man. The idea was often expressed in the poetry of Shakespeare's age, but nowhere is it worked out so fully and with so much liveliness. Each age of man's life is represented by a character who, in a few words of description, comes completely to life. The dramatic reason for this long speech is to allow time for Orlando to go away and return with Adam.

86 *exits . . . entrances*, i.e. deaths and births.

87 *plays many parts:* A man is regarded as a different "character" in the "play" of life according to his age.

88 *His acts . . . ages* – "the seven ages of his life being described in seven acts".

89 *Mewling and puking* – "crying and being sick".

90 *shining morning face*, i.e. shining from its morning wash.

91 *woeful ballad Made to* – "very sad poem written in praise of".

92 *bearded like the pard* – "with a beard like the rough hair of a leopard *(pard)*".

93 *Jealous in honour* – "always anxious to defend his honour (as a soldier)".

94 *Seeking . . . cannon's mouth*, i.e. going close to the enemy's positions *(cannon*, big gun on wheels) to try to get a reputation for bravery, although such a reputation has no real value and does not last longer than a bubble of soapy water.

95 *justice* – "judge" (or "justice of the peace", not trained in the law but able to decide less important cases) – usually a middle-aged man.

96 *In fair . . . lined* – "with a fine round stomach filled with the best meat of the *capon* (cock fattened for eating)". (Justices were forbidden to take bribes, but it was a common practice for poor men to bring capons as presents when their cases were tried.)

97 *of formal cut* – "carefully cut" (as was suitable for an important man).

98 *Full of . . . instances* – "(his conversation) filled with old wise sayings *(saws)* and ordinary dull examples".

99 *And so . . . his part:* There is a double meaning here: not only is the justice another actor on the stage of life; he is also "playing a part" in pretending to be more virtuous than he really is.

100 *shifts Into . . . pantaloon* – "changes to another character of the play, the lean, laughable, feeble old man in slippers". *Pantaloon* was the name given to such characters in Italian comedies of that time.

101 *pouch on side* – "purse (hanging from his belt) at his side".

102 *youthful hose . . . shank* – "leg garments *(hose)* made for him when he was a young man, and carefully mended *(saved)*, a great deal too wide for his leg *(shrank)*, which has grown thin and bony *(shrunk)*".

DUKE SENIOR

Go find him out,
And we will nothing waste[82] till you return.

ORLANDO

I thank ye; and be blest for your good comfort!   [*Exit*

DUKE SENIOR

Thou seest we are not all alone[83] unhappy: 135
This wide and universal theatre[84]
Presents more woeful pageants[85] than the scene
Wherein we play in.

JAQUES

All the world 's a stage,
And all the men and women merely players:
They have their exits[86] and their entrances,   140
And one man in his time plays many parts,[87]
His acts being seven ages.[88] At first, the infant,
Mewling[89] and puking in the nurse's arms.
Then the whining schoolboy, with his satchel
And shining morning face,[90] creeping like snail   145
Unwillingly to school. And then the lover,
Sighing like furnace, with a woeful ballad[91]
Made to his mistress' eyebrow. Then a soldier,
Full of strange oaths, and bearded like the pard,[92]
Jealous in honour,[93] sudden and quick in quarrel,   150
Seeking the bubble[94] reputation
Even in the cannon's mouth. And then the justice,[95]
In fair round belly[96] with good capon lined,
With eyes severe and beard of formal cut,[97]
Full of wise saws[98] and modern instances;   155
And so he plays his part.[99] The sixth age shifts[100]
Into the lean and slippered pantaloon,
With spectacles on nose and pouch[101] on side,
His youthful hose,[102] well saved, a world too wide

95

103 *Turning ... sound* – "changing back towards the high-pitched voice *(treble)* of a child, makes a weak piping and whistling sound (when he talks)".

104 *mere oblivion* – "complete forgetfulness" (of all that has happened).

105 *Sans* – "without".

106 *venerable*, i.e. deserving respect because of his age.

107 *So had you need:* Adam is grateful to Orlando for saying the thanks (for the welcome and offer of food) which Adam himself is too weak to say properly.

108 *fall to* – "start eating".

109 *unkind* – "unnatural and cruel".

110 *Thy tooth ... not seen* – "your bite is not so sharp because you are not a person who can be seen". Duke Senior, with the help of his friends, ruled as fairly and kindly as they could in the country from which they are now banished because of "man's ingratitude". They have learnt in Arden that nature's cruelty is not so bad as the cruelty of an ungrateful man, whose unkindness is personal, not, like the wind's, impersonal.

111 *rude* – "rough".

112 *Heigh-ho*, an expression of joy. In the same line, *holly* names a plant which was used as a sign of joy.

113 *feigning* – "deceiving".

the lean and slippered pantaloon

96

For his shrunk shank, and his big manly voice,   160
Turning again toward childish treble,[103] pipes
And whistles in his sound. Last scene of all,
That ends this strange eventful history,
Is second childishness and mere oblivion,[104]
Sans[105] teeth, sans eyes, sans taste, sans everything.   165

Enter ORLANDO *carrying* ADAM

DUKE SENIOR

Welcome. Set down your venerable[106] burden,
And let him feed.

ORLANDO

I thank you most for him.

ADAM

[*To* ORLANDO] So had you need;[107]
[*To* DUKE SENIOR] I scarce can speak to thank you for myself.

DUKE SENIOR

Welcome, fall to:[108] I will not trouble you   170
As yet, to question you about your fortunes.
Give us some music; and, good cousin, sing.

AMIENS [*Sings*]

Blow, blow thou winter wind,
Thou art not so unkind[109]
　　As man's ingratitude;   175
Thy tooth[110] is not so keen,
Because thou art not seen,
　　Although thy breath be rude.[111]
Heigh-ho,[112] sing heigh-ho, unto the green holly;
Most friendship is feigning,[113] most loving mere folly: 180
Then, heigh-ho, the holly!
This life is most jolly.

97

114 *bitter sky*, i.e. sky from which the wind blows bitterly cold.

115 *so nigh* – "so close" (to the bone, perhaps).

116 *warp* – "change the form" (by turning into ice or blowing into waves).

117 *As you have . . . you were*: Orlando has been in whispered conversation with Duke Senior while Amiens was singing.

118 *as mine eye . . . your face*, i.e. Orlando's face is so exactly like his father's (as Duke Senior remembers it) that he could be a painting of his father (*effigies* – "painting, likeness"; *limned* – "drawn").

119 *The residue . . . tell me* – "come into my cave to tell me about the rest *(residue)* of your adventures *(fortune)*".

120 *right* – "very".

121 *let me . . . understand*, i.e. tell me about everything that has happened to you.

Freeze, freeze, thou bitter sky,[114]
That dost not bite so nigh[115]
 As benefits forgot: 185
Though thou the waters warp,[116]
Thy sting is not so sharp
 As friend remembered not.
Heigh-ho, sing heigh-ho, unto the green holly:
Most friendship is feigning, most loving mere folly: 190
Then, heigh-ho, the holly!
This life is most jolly.

DUKE SENIOR

If that you were the good Sir Rowland's son,
As you have whispered[117] faithfully you were,
And as mine eye[118] doth his effigies witness   195
Most truly limned and living in your face,
Be truly welcome hither. I am the Duke
That loved your father. The residue[119] of your fortune
Go to my cave and tell me. Good old man,
Thou art right[120] welcome, as thy master is.   200
Support him by the arm. Give me your hand,
And let me all your fortunes[121] understand.

           [*Exeunt*

(III.i) Oliver has been brought to the court. Duke Frederick orders him to find Orlando, and meanwhile seizes all Oliver's land and property.

1 *Not see him since:* As they come in, Duke Frederick and Oliver are in the middle of a conversation. Oliver has said that he has not seen Orlando since the day of the wrestling match.

2 *were I not . . . mercy* – "if my character were not mostly made up of mercy". (No one is likely to believe this description of Duke Frederick by himself.)

3 *I should not . . . present* – "I should have revenge on you, who are present, instead of seeking an object for my revenge who is absent". Duke Frederick wants revenge because he thinks that Orlando helped his daughter to run away. He could be revenged on the family by punishing Oliver, but he is "merciful".

4 *look to it* – "take care".

5 *Seek him with candle* – "look for him as closely as you would search with a candle for something missing in the dark".

6 *Within this twelvemonth* – "in less than one year from now".

7 *do we seize . . . hands* – "I take formal possession of them". As a ruler, Duke Frederick uses *we* instead of *I*, *our* instead of *my*, etc.

8 *quit thee . . . mouth* – "clear yourself of blame through what your brother has to say".

9 *what we think against thee*, i.e. that Oliver encouraged Orlando to escape.

10 *More villain thou* – "That makes you an even worse villain".

11 *let my officers . . . extent upon* – "tell the officers whose duty it is to do such work to go and seize".

12 *expediently* – "speedily".

13 *turn him going* – "get rid of him (Oliver)".

100

ACT III

Scene I. The palace.

Enter DUKE FREDERICK, *Lords, and* OLIVER *guarded by Attendants.*

DUKE FREDERICK

Not see him since?[1] Sir, sir, that cannot be:
But were I not the better part[2] made mercy,
I should not seek an absent argument[3]
Of my revenge, thou present. But look to it:[4]
Find out thy brother, wheresoe'er he is;   5
Seek him with candle;[5] bring him dead or living,
Within this twelvemonth,[6] or turn thou no more
To seek a living in our territory.
Thy lands, and all things that thou dost call thine
Worth seizure, do we seize[7] into our hands,   10
Till thou canst quit[8] thee by thy brother's mouth
Of what we think against thee.[9]

OLIVER

O that your Highness knew my heart in this!
I never loved my brother in my life.

DUKE FREDERICK

More villain thou.[10] [*To the Attendants*] Well, push him out
   of doors,   15
And let my officers of such a nature[11]
Make an extent upon this house and lands.
Do this expediently[12] and turn him going.[13]

                                                                                   [*Exeunt*

101

(III.ii) This is the central scene of the play. Orlando hangs on a tree his verses in praise of Rosalind. Touchstone and Corin compare the shepherd's life with the life at court. Rosalind reads Orlando's verses, and Touchstone makes fun of the kind of love described by poets, adding a poem of his own. Celia comes to them and tells Rosalind that she has seen Orlando in the forest. The two girls hear a conversation between Orlando and Jaques, who mocks Orlando for being in love. Rosalind, in her disguise, steps forward and speaks to Orlando. She offers to cure him of his love if he will come to her every day and pretend to woo her.

1 *Hang there:* He fastens to a tree the paper on which his poem is written. Lines 1–10, where Orlando speaks of his verse, are themselves written in rhyming verse in the style of a sonnet except that a proper sonnet would have four more lines.

2 *thrice-crownéd . . . night,* i.e. the moon. In the Greek and Roman religions the moon goddess was a queen in three ways: as queen of heaven, queen of the underworld, and queen of hunting on earth. The last is the important one here although in the rest of the scene it does not appear to be night. Orlando calls on her, as the virgin goddess, to look down from her place in the sky to see *(survey)* the pure virgin (Rosalind) whose love rules *(doth sway)* his life (as the heavenly bodies were supposed to rule men's lives).

3 *pale sphere:* Like the stars, the moon was thought to move in a sphere (see II,vii.6 and note on it), as pale as the moon's light.

4 *Thy huntress' name,* i.e. the name *Rosalind* in the poem hanging on the tree. Because Rosalind was a pure virgin *(chaste),* Orlando thought of her as favoured by the moon, the queen of hunting, and so called her one of Diana's huntresses.

5 *character* – "carve in letters".

6 *thy virtue witnessed* – "proof of your power", i.e. the fact that the name *Rosalind* is carved on every tree will prove to anyone in the forest that she is supreme.

7 *unexpressive* – "beyond description" (her perfection cannot be expressed in words).

8 *in respect of itself* – "as far as it is the life of a shepherd".

9 *in respect that . . . naught* – "as far as it is a shepherd's life, it is bad *(naught)*". In this speech Touchstone expresses two contrary opinions about everything in the shepherd's life, so that what he says at first seems nonsense, but see Introduction, p. xv.

10 *spare* – "simple and hard".

11 *fits my humour* – "agrees with what I like".

12 *plenty* – "wealth".

13 *goes much . . . stomach* – "is not at all what I like".

14 *Hast any . . . thee* – "Do you know any philosophy".

15 *No more but* – "Only".

16 *worse at ease* – "less comfortable".

17 *wants* – "lacks".

18 *property* – "special quality".

Scene II. The forest.

Enter ORLANDO *with a sheet of paper in his hand.*

ORLANDO

Hang there,[1] my verse, in witness of my love;
   And thou, thrice-crownéd queen of night,[2] survey
With thy chaste eye, from thy pale sphere[3] above,
   Thy huntress'[4] name that my full life doth sway.
O Rosalind! These trees shall be my books,   5
   And in their barks my thoughts I'll character,[5]
That every eye which in this forest looks
   Shall see thy virtue witnessed[6] everywhere.
Run, run, Orlando; carve on every tree
The fair, the chaste, and unexpressive[7] she.   *[Exit* 10

Enter CORIN *and* TOUCHSTONE

CORIN

And how like you this shepherd's life, Master Touchstone?

TOUCHSTONE

Truly, shepherd, in respect of itself,[8] it is a good life; but in
respect that[9] it is a shepherd's life, it is naught. In respect that it
is solitary, I like it very well; but in respect that it is private, it
is a very vile life. Now, in respect it is in the fields, it pleaseth   15
me well; but in respect it is not in the court, it is tedious. As it is
a spare[10] life, look you, it fits my humour[11] well; but as there is
no more plenty[12] in it, it goes much against[13] my stomach. Hast
any philosophy[14] in thee, shepherd?

CORIN

No more, but[15] that I know the more one sickens, the worse at   20
ease[16] he is; and that he that wants[17] money, means, and content
is without three good friends; that the property[18] of rain is to
wet, and fire to burn; that good pasture makes fat sheep; and

19 *art* – "study".

20 *complain . . . kindred* – "complain with good reason that he has not been brought up well, or else he comes from a very unintelligent family".

21 *natural philosopher:* This was the sixteenth-century name for a scientist, but of course Touchstone is playing with another meaning of *natural* – a born fool.

22 *like an ill-roasted . . . side* – "like an egg that is so badly cooked that it is done only on one side" (i.e. Corin's knowledge, taken from nature without courtly manners, is one-sided).

23 *thy manners must be wicked:* Touchstone is playing with an older meaning of *manners* – "moral character".

24 *parlous* – "dangerous" (an Elizabethan way of spelling "perilous").

25 *Not a whit* – "Not in the least".

26 *you salute not . . . hands* – "at court you do not greet each other *(salute)* without kissing hands".

27 *courtesy* – "way of showing good manners".

that a great cause of the night is lack of the sun; that he that
hath learned no wit by nature nor art[19] may complain[20] of good   25
breeding, or comes of a very dull kindred.

TOUCHSTONE

Such a one is a natural[21] philosopher. Wast ever in court,
shepherd?

CORIN

No, truly.

TOUCHSTONE

Then thou art damned.   30

CORIN

Nay, I hope.

TOUCHSTONE

Truly thou art damned, like an ill-roasted[22] egg, all on one side.

CORIN

For not being at court? Your reason.

TOUCHSTONE

Why, if thou never wast at court, thou never sawest good
manners; if thou never sawest good manners, then thy manners   35
must be wicked;[23] and wickedness is sin, and sin is damnation.
Thou art in a parlous[24] state, shepherd.

CORIN

Not a whit,[25] Touchstone: those that are good manners at the
court are as ridiculous in the country as the behaviour of the
country is most mockable at the court. You told me you salute   40
not[26] at the court but you kiss your hands; that courtesy[27] would
be uncleanly, if courtiers were shepherds.

28 *Instance* – "Give (me) proof (of that)".

29 *still handling* – "always touching (with our hands)".

30 *your courtier's* – "a courtier's".

31 *mutton* – "sheep".

32 *Shallow* – "A weak, unsatisfying answer".

33 *more sounder instance* – "stronger proof".

34 *the surgery* – "healing the wounds" (which the shepherds did by applying tar).

35 *Thou worms' meat . . . flesh* – "You (who are fit only to be) food for worms as compared with good flesh (i.e. a good man)".

36 *perpend* – "consider".

37 *baser birth* – "worse origin".

38 *uncleanly . . . cat* – "unclean liquid matter produced by the organs of a (civet) cat" (see *civet* in Glossary).

39 *Mend the instance* – "Give a better proof".

40 *rest* – "give up". Touchstone seems to have won the argument, but only by showing that shepherds are cleaner than courtiers.

41 *damned*, i.e. for not having been at court – see lines 27–37.

42 *make incision . . . raw* – "cut you up (so that you can be well cooked). You are unfinished". Touchstone now speaks as if Corin were one of his own sheep – not the *ill-roasted egg* of line 32. He uses *raw* in two senses: (i) "uncooked" (meat); and (ii) "uneducated".

TOUCHSTONE

Instance,[28] briefly; come, instance.

CORIN

Why, we are still[29] handling our ewes, and their fells, you know,
are greasy.   45

TOUCHSTONE

Why, do not your[30] courtier's hands sweat? And is not the grease
of a mutton[31] as wholesome as the sweat of a man? Shallow,[32]
shallow. A better instance, I say; come.

CORIN

Besides, our hands are hard.

TOUCHSTONE

Your lips will feel them the sooner. Shallow again. A more   50
sounder[33] instance, come.

CORIN

And they are often tarred over with the surgery[34] of our sheep;
and would you have us kiss tar? The courtier's hands are perfumed with civet.

TOUCHSTONE

Most shallow man! Thou worms' meat[35] in respect of a good   55
piece of flesh, indeed! Learn of the wise, and perpend.[36] Civet
is of a baser birth[37] than tar, the very uncleanly flux[38] of a cat.
Mend the instance,[39] shepherd.

CORIN

You have too courtly a wit for me; I 'll rest.[40]

TOUCHSTONE

Wilt thou rest damned?[41] God help thee, shallow man! God   60
make incision[42] in thee! Thou art raw.

43 *that* – "that which"; "what".

44 *get* – "gain by work".

45 *good* – "good fortune".

46 *content with my harm* – "accept my own difficulties cheerfully".

47 *simple sin*, i.e. wrong action of a simple man.

48 *offer* – "be willing".

49 *copulation of cattle* – "bringing sheep together for the purpose of breeding".

50 *bawd* – "agent for immoral purposes".

51 *crooked-pated ... match* – "foolish and easily deceived *(cuckoldly)* old male sheep with crooked horns, which is not at all a fair *(reasonable)* marriage".

52 *thou beest* – "you are".

53 *the devil . . . 'scape* – "(it will be because) the devil (who controls hell, the place of punishment for the *damned*) refuses to receive any shepherds; otherwise I can see no reason why you should escape going to hell".

54 *the east . . . Ind* – "the East Indies to the West Indies".

55 *like* – "as precious as".

56 *Her worth ... wind* – "her reputation, carried by the wind".

57 *bears* – "carries the fame of".

58 *fairest lined . . . black to* – "most beautifully drawn are ugly by comparison with".

59 *fair* – "lovely face".

60 *rhyme you . . . together* – "make rhymes for you like these for eight years without stopping".

61 *it is the right . . . market*, i.e. line follows line, each with the same rhyme, like village women riding one after another in a line *(rank)*, going to sell their butter in the market (in the nearest town).

62 *Out* – "be quiet".

CORIN

Sir, I am a true labourer; I earn that[43] I eat, get[44] that I wear,
owe no man hate, envy no man's happiness, glad of other men's
good,[45] content with my harm;[46] and the greatest of my pride
is to see my ewes graze and my lambs suck.   65

TOUCHSTONE

That is another simple sin[47] in you: to bring the ewes and the
rams together, and to offer[48] to get your living by the copulation[49] of cattle; to be bawd[50] to a bell-wether, and to betray
a she-lamb of a twelve-month to a crooked-pated,[51] old,
cuckoldly ram, out of all reasonable match. If thou beest[52] not   70
damned for this, the devil himself[53] will have no shepherds; I
cannot see else how thou shouldst 'scape.

CORIN

Here comes young Master Ganymede, my new mistress's brother.

Enter ROSALIND, *reading a sheet of paper*

ROSALIND

> *From the east to western Ind,[54]*
> *No jewel is like[55] Rosalind.*   75
> *Her worth,[56] being mounted on the wind*
> *Through all the world bears[57] Rosalind.*
> *All the pictures fairest lined[58]*
> *Are but black to Rosalind.*
> *Let no face be kept in mind*   80
> *But the fair[59] of Rosalind.*

TOUCHSTONE

I 'll rhyme[60] you so eight years together, dinners and suppers
and sleeping hours excepted: it is the right butter-women's[61]
rank to market.

ROSALIND

Out,[62] fool!   85

109

63 *For a taste* – "Here is an example".

64 *will after kind* – "will seek another cat".

65 *Winter . . . lined* – "Garments for use in winter must have a warm lining".

66 *sheaf and bind* – "gather the corn into bundles and tie *(bind)* them".

67 *to cart with*, i.e. put her on the cart like cut corn and take her away (to a husband).

68 *rind* – "outer covering".

69 *love's prick* – "the pain of love" (like the thorn that grows with the rose).

70 *very false . . . verses* – "quite the worst kind of verse" (the image is of a horse that canters – half galloping and half trotting – not properly under control). Touchstone is describing Orlando's poem and his own imitation of it.

71 *infect yourself* – "let yourself be troubled".

72 *graff*, for *graft* – see Glossary. Rosalind is playing with words – *you* and *yew* (a kind of tree); *medlar* (a kind of fruit which decays as soon as it is ripe) and *meddler* (a person who is always interfering in other people's business).

73 *right virtue* – "typical quality".

74 *said* – "spoken (your opinion)".

75 *let . . . judge* – "let those who live in the forest (and know the ways of nature) judge who is right". Touchstone means that the description of Rosalind in his rhymes is true, although it has made her angry. Her love is not really different from that of all natural creatures.

TOUCHSTONE

For a taste:[63]

> If a hart do lack a hind,
> Let him seek out Rosalind.
> If the cat will after kind,[64]
> So be sure will Rosalind.   90
> Winter[65] garments must be lined,
> So must slender Rosalind.
> They that reap must sheaf[66] and bind,
> Then to cart[67] with Rosalind.
> Sweetest nut hath sourest rind,[68]   95
> Such a nut is Rosalind.
> He that sweetest rose will find
> Must find love's prick, and Rosalind.

This[69] is the very false gallop of verses:[70] why do you infect
yourself[71] with them?   100

ROSALIND

Peace, you dull fool! I found them on a tree.

TOUCHSTONE

Truly the tree yields bad fruit.

ROSALIND

I 'll graff[72] it with you, and then I shall graff it with a medlar.
Then it will be the earliest fruit i' th' country; for you 'll be
rotten ere you be half ripe, and that 's the right virtue[73] of the 105
medlar.

TOUCHSTONE

You have said;[74] but whether wisely or no, let[75] the forest
judge.

Enter CELIA *holding another sheet of paper*

111

76 *a desert* – "an empty place".

77 *For it is unpeopled* – "Because it is un-inhabited".

78 *Tongues*, i.e. writings.

79 *civil sayings* – "such things as civilised people say".

80 *Some, how . . . sum of age* – "some (will say) how short and full of mistakes *(erring)* is man's life (seen as a pilgrim's journey towards heaven), so that all the years he lives *(his sum of age)* are so few that they could be held in one hand" *(span*, the distance measured by the greatest width of a hand fully spread out; *buckles in* – "marks the limit of").

81 *violated vows* – "broken promises".

82 *'Twixt*, for *Betwixt* – "between".

83 *Rosalinda*: Italian form of *Rosalind*, chosen here to make a regular line (see Introduction, p. xxii).

84 *quintessence . . . in little show* – "purest essence of the human spirit *(sprite)* that heaven wanted to show in a small space", i.e. Rosalind shows in one person all that makes up the best qualities in human beings.

85 *Heaven Nature charged* – "heaven gave orders to Nature (personified)".

86 *wide-enlarged* – "fully developed".

87 *presently distilled* – "immediately drew out the essence (from)". Orlando's poem claims (lines 126–35) that Nature, obeying heaven's command, has combined Helen's beauty, Cleopatra's majesty, Atalanta's virgin grace, and Lucretia's modesty, all in the person of Rosalind.

88 *Helen's cheek, but not her heart*: The ancient Greeks thought Helen the most beautiful woman in the world, but not the most virtuous. She was false to her husband Menelaus, and by running away with Paris of Troy, she caused the long war between Greeks and Trojans. In Orlando's line, *cheek* (face) stands for beauty which can be seen, *heart* for

unseen qualities of character. Rosalind has Helen's beauty only; her *heart* is more virtuous than Helen's.

89 *Cleopatra's majesty*, i.e. the royal manner of the great queen of ancient Egypt, whose unhappy love and death are the subject of Shakespeare's play *Antony and Cleopatra*.

90 *Atalanta's better part*: Atalanta, according to Greek literature, was a great virgin huntress and runner. Her *better part* would be her grace and quickness of movement, not the greed suggested by one story about her.

91 *Sad Lucretia's modesty*: Lucretia was a true wife who died rather than be unfaithful to her husband. Shakespeare's poem *Lucrece* tells this ancient Roman story.

92 *By heavenly . . . devised* – "was planned *(devised)* by (the decision of) the assembly *(synod)* of heaven". The idea is that the gods, meeting in the heaven of the ancients, agreed that one perfect human being – Rosalind – should be made from the best qualities of all these famous women.

93 *the touches . . . prized* – "the most highly valued *(prized)* qualities".

94 *would* – "wished".

112

ROSALIND

Peace! Here comes my sister, reading: stand aside.

> [ROSALIND, TOUCHSTONE, *and* CORIN
> *stand behind a tree while* CELIA *reads*

CELIA

Why should this a desert[76] *be?*	110
For it is unpeopled?[77] *No:*	
Tongues[78] *I 'll hang on every tree,*	
That shall civil sayings[79] *show:*	
Some, how[80] *brief the life of man*	
Runs his erring pilgrimage,	115
That the stretching of a span	
Buckles in his sum of age;	
Some, of violated vows[81]	
'Twixt[82] *the souls of friend and friend;*	
But upon the fairest boughs,	120
Or at every sentence end,	
Will I "Rosalinda"[83] *write,*	
Teaching all that read to know	
The quintessence[84] *of every sprite*	
Heaven would in little show.	125
Therefore Heaven Nature[85] *charged*	
That one body should be filled	
With all graces wide-enlarged.[86]	
Nature presently distilled[87]	
Helen's cheek,[88] *but not her heart,*	130
Cleopatra's majesty,[89]	
Atalanta's better part,[90]	
Sad Lucretia's modesty.[91]	
Thus Rosalind of many parts	
By heavenly synod[92] *was devised;*	135
Of many faces, eyes, and hearts,	
To have the touches[93] *dearest prized.*	
Heaven would[94] *that she these gifts should have,*	
And to live and die her slave.	

95 *pulpiter* – "preacher".

96 *what tedious . . . withal* – "what a boring sermon *(homily)* about love you have wearied the local people in your church *(parishioners)* with".

97 *Have patience . . . people*, the cry of preachers when listeners were getting tired.

98 *sirrah*, the usual form of address to a manservant.

99 *though not with . . . scrippage* – "we cannot take all our possessions *(bag and baggage*, i.e. bag and what it contains), but at least we can take something" (perhaps he picks up the paper Celia has dropped and put it in his *scrip*, or leather bag; this would be *scrippage*, a word he invents to balance *baggage*).

100 *more feet . . . bear:* Each line, or "verse", of the poem should have a regular number of "feet", i.e. units each containing one beat (see Introduction, p. xxi). Rosalind says (in fact, she is wrong) that Orlando's poem sometimes had too many feet in one line. In the two speeches that follow, Celia and Rosalind play on the two meanings of *feet*: as verse units and as the "feet" that walk.

101 *lame:* In verse a *lame* foot does not follow the regular beat of the lines and prevents the poem from being smoothly read.

102 *wondering* – "surprise".

103 *I was seven . . . wonder:* The common saying "a nine days' wonder" shows the longest time the surprise caused by any event is supposed to last. Rosalind says that she has been through seven days of the nine, i.e. she has almost got over her surprise.

104 *so berhymed* – "the subject of so many rhymes".

105 *since Pythagoras' . . . rat* – "since the time when Pythagoras lived, when I may have been an Irish rat". Rosalind plays here with two ideas. (1) Pythagoras, the Greek philosopher, taught that souls passed at death into another body, either human or animal. (2) Irish magicians, it was said, could cause rats to die by reciting magic rhymes. If Rosalind had once, in another life, been an Irish rat, she might have had as many rhymes directed at her by magicians as Orlando is now writing in her praise.

*most gentle pulpiter*95

114

ROSALIND [*stepping forward*]

O most gentle pulpiter,[95] what tedious homily[96] of love have   140
you wearied your parishioners withal, and never cried, "Have
patience, good people!"[97]

CELIA

How now! Back friends. Shepherd, go off a little. [*To* TOUCH-
STONE] Go with him, sirrah.[98]

TOUCHSTONE

Come, shepherd, let us make an honourable retreat; though not   145
with bag and baggage,[99] yet with scrip and scrippage.
                    [*Exeunt* TOUCHSTONE *and* CORIN

CELIA

Didst thou hear these verses?

ROSALIND

O, yes, I heard them all, and more too; for some of them had in
them more feet[100] than the verses would bear.

CELIA

That 's no matter; the feet might bear the verses.   150

ROSALIND

Ay, but the feet were lame,[101] and could not bear themselves
without the verse, and therefore stood lamely in the verse.

CELIA

But didst thou hear without wondering,[102] how thy name should
be hanged and carved upon these trees?

ROSALIND

I was seven of the nine days[103] out of the wonder before you   155
came; for look here, what I found on a palm tree. I was never
so berhymed[104] since Pythagoras' time,[105] that I was an Irish rat,
which I can hardly remember.

106 *Trow you* – "Do you know".

107 *And a chain* – "(Yes) and with a chain" (see I.ii.200).

108 *Change your colour* – "Is your face getting red (because I mention this)?"

109 *a hard matter . . . encounter* – "not at all easy for friends to meet, although (it may happen, just as) earthquakes may cause mountains to move and so meet *(encounter)* each other". Celia avoids answering Rosalind directly, so that she might have the pleasure of keeping Rosalind curious. Her indirect answer means that it is not impossible for Orlando to be in the forest.

110 *Is it possible*, i.e. Does Rosalind really need to be told?

111 *with . . . vehemence* – "begging for an answer as hard as I can".

112 *out of all hooping* – "more (surprising) than would (ordinarily) make one cry out". (Sometimes printed *whooping*.)

113 *Good my complexion* – "Oh, my *blushes* (becoming red through shyness, thus changing the colouring of the face, the *complexion*)".

114 *caparisoned . . . disposition* – "dressed up like a man, that I have a man's nature *(disposition)*". For *doublet and hose*, a man's clothes, see p. 66, note 3.

115 *One inch . . . discovery* – "the least delay feels like a great stretch of time". The South Seas were just then being discovered; Rosalind's metaphor refers to the enormously long voyages involved in that discovery.

116 *apace* – "as fast as you can".

CELIA

Trow[106] you who hath done this?

ROSALIND

Is it a man?   160

CELIA

And a chain,[107] that you once wore, about his neck. Change you colour?[108]

ROSALIND

I prithee, who?

CELIA

O Lord, Lord, it is a hard matter[109] for friends to meet; but mountains may be removed with earthquakes, and so encounter. 165

ROSALIND

Nay, but who is it?

CELIA

Is it possible?[110]

ROSALIND

Nay, I prithee now with most petitionary vehemence,[111] tell me who it is.

CELIA

O wonderful, wonderful, and most wonderful wonderful, and 170 yet again wonderful, and after that, out of all hooping![112]

ROSALIND

Good my complexion![113] Dost thou think, though I am caparisoned[114] like a man, I have a doublet and hose in my disposition? One inch of delay[115] more is a South Sea of discovery; I prithee, tell me who is it quickly, and speak apace.[116] I would thou 175

117

117 *this concealed man* – "(the name of) this man that you are hiding from me".

118 *take . . . mouth*, i.e. speak up (still using the image of the bottle).

119 *drink thy tidings* – "take in your news".

120 *So you . . . man*, i.e. by taking in news of a man as one drinks wine.

121 *Is he . . . making* – "Is he naturally manly" (or only manly-looking because of his clothes, i.e. of the tailor's making).

122 *Is his head . . . worth a beard*, i.e. is his head good-looking enough to deserve a hat, and his chin so well shaped as to deserve a beard? (Or are the hat and the beard hiding his faults?)

123 *but* – "only".

124 *let me stay . . . chin* – "I can wait for his beard to grow, but you must not keep me waiting to know whose chin it is".

125 *the devil take mocking* – "stop making fun of me".

126 *Speak sad . . . maid* – "Speak seriously *(sad brow)*, as is right for a truthful girl".

127 *I' faith* – "Indeed".

couldst stammer, that thou mightst pour this concealed man[117]
out of thy mouth, as wine comes out of a narrow-mouthed
bottle, either too much at once, or none at all. I prithee take the
cork[118] out of thy mouth, that I may drink thy tidings.[119]

CELIA

So you may put a man[120] in your belly.   180

ROSALIND

Is he of God's making[121] What manner of man? Is his head[122]
worth a hat? Or his chin worth a beard?

CELIA

Nay, he hath but[123] a little beard.

ROSALIND

Why, God will send more, if the man will be thankful: let me
stay[124] the growth of his beard, if thou delay me not the know- 185
ledge of his chin.

CELIA

It is young Orlando, that tripped up the wrestler's heels and
your heart, both in an instant.

ROSALIND

Nay, but the devil take[125] mocking! Speak sad brow[126] and true
maid.   190

CELIA

I' faith,[127] coz, 't is he.

ROSALIND

Orlando?

CELIA

Orlando.

128 *Alas the day* – "At what an unfortunate time". (Rosalind's first thought is that Orlando will now see her dressed in man's clothes.)

129 *did he* – "was he doing".

130 *Wherein went he* – "What clothes was he wearing".

131 *makes he* – "is he doing" (i.e. is his purpose in being here).

132 *in one word* – "at once (and without wasting words)". Celia pretends to understand this as a demand for a one-word answer to all Rosalind's questions together.

133 *Gargantua* was a giant (person of more than human size) in very old French stories and also in books written by Rabelais in 1532 and 1534. Gargantua's mouth was very big; he once swallowed five pilgrims in a mouthful of food.

134 *of this age's size* – "of the small size that people's mouths are in our time".

135 *particulars* – "detailed questions".

136 *freshly* – "healthy".

137 *count atomies . . . lover* – "count grains of dust (from which comes our word 'atoms') as to answer (all) the questions of a lover".

138 *take a taste . . . observance* – "feed your curiosity a little by hearing how I found him, and enjoy *(relish)* it by paying careful attention".

139 *Jove's tree*, i.e. the finest tree, since Jove was the greatest of the ancient gods.

140 *Give me . . . madam:* To mock Rosalind, Celia used the courtly language spoken before a queen. In plain words: "Listen to me".

141 *along* – "at full length".

142 *well becomes the ground*, i.e. makes the ground look more beautiful (becomes – "suits").

You must borrow me Gargantua's[133] *mouth first*

ROSALIND

Alas the day![128] What shall I do with my doublet and hose?
What did he[129] when thou sawest him? What said he? How 195
looked he? Wherein went[130] he? What makes[131] he here? Did he
ask for me? Where remains he? How parted he with thee? And
when shalt thou see him again? Answer me in one word.[132]

CELIA

You must borrow me Gargantua's[133] mouth first; 'tis a word too
great for any mouth of this age's[134] size. To say Ay and No to 200
these particulars[135] is more than to answer in a catechism.

ROSALIND

But doth he know that I am in this forest, and in man's apparel?
Looks he as freshly[136] as he did the day he wrestled?

CELIA

It is as easy to count atomies[137] as to resolve the propositions
of a lover; but take a taste[138] of my finding him, and relish 205
it with good observance. I found him under a tree, like a dropped
acorn.

ROSALIND

It may well be called Jove's tree,[139] when it drops such fruit.

CELIA

Give me audience,[140] good madam.

ROSALIND

Proceed. 210

CELIA

There lay he, stretched along,[141] like a wounded knight.

ROSALIND

Though it be pity to see such a sight, it well becomes[142] the
ground.

143 *Cry "holla" to thy tongue* – "Call your tongue to stop running on". *Holla* was the call to a horse when it did not stop immediately. Celia's image of the badly controlled horse continues in *curvets* – "jumps about" (like a restless horse).

144 *unseasonably* – "at the wrong time".

145 *furnished* – "dressed".

146 *heart*, with word-play on *hart* (deer), since Orlando looked like a hunter.

147 *I would . . . tune* – "I should like to sing my song (i.e. give my description) without anybody joining in (i.e. without interruptions); you are making me sing (i.e. tell) it badly".

148 *bring me out* – "are upsetting the story" (as *bringest me out of tune*, line 218).

149 *Soft* – "(We must) be quiet".

150 *Slink by . . . him* – "(Let us) slip away quietly and watch him". (Rosalind and Celia are not seen by Orlando and Jaques during the conversation which follows.)

151 *good faith . . . alone* – "indeed, I should as gladly *(lief)* have been alone".

152 *for fashion sake* – "for the sake of good manners".

153 *society* – "company".

154 *God buy you* – "God be with you" (meaning the same as "Good-bye").

155 *be better strangers* – "become increasingly strangers" (changing round the usual polite wish to be "better acquainted").

CELIA

Cry "holla"[143] to thy tongue, I prithee; it curvets[144] unseasonably. He was furnished[145] like a hunter.   215

ROSALIND

O, ominous! He comes to kill my heart.[146]

CELIA

I would sing my song without a burden;[147] thou bring'st me out
of tune.

ROSALIND

Do you not know I am a woman? When I think, I must speak.
Sweet, say on.   220

Enter ORLANDO *and* JAQUES

CELIA

You bring me out:[148] Soft![149] Comes he not here?

ROSALIND

'T is he! Slink by,[150] and note him.   [*They stand back*

JAQUES

[*To* ORLANDO] I thank you for your company; but, good
faith,[151] I had as lief have been myself alone.

ORLANDO

And so had I; but yet for fashion sake[152] I thank you too for 225
your society.[153]

JAQUES

God buy you;[154] let 's meet as little as we can.

ORLANDO

I do desire we may be better strangers.[155]

156 *no moe . . . ill-favouredly* – "no more of my poems by reading them unpleasingly".

157 *just* – "(you are) quite right".

158 *What stature . . . of?* – "What is her height?"

159 *Just as . . . heart*, i.e. just tall enough for Orlando to love her.

160 *goldsmiths' wives*, wives of the makers of gold objects; the richest and best-dressed ladies of the merchant class; many young nobles liked to make their acquaintance.

161 *conned . . . rings*, i.e. learnt them (the "pretty answers") from the words cut inside finger rings made by goldsmiths for lovers. (Shakespeare's *The Merchant of Venice* has an example in v.i.149 of a message carved inside a ring: "Love me, and leave me not.")

162 *right painted cloth*, i.e. using the words painted with the pictures on cloths which were often hung up to brighten the walls of inns. The words were usually well-known sayings, containing no new ideas.

163 *from whence . . . questions*, meaning that Jaques has learnt such questions while wasting time in inns (a smart reply to Jaques's claim that Orlando learnt his answers while talking to and spending money with goldsmiths' wives).

164 *nimble wit* – "quick mind".

165 *Atalanta's heels:* See p. 112, note 90.

166 *rail . . . world* – "complain about the ways of the world, as if it were a cruel mistress".

Atalanta

JAQUES

I pray you mar no more trees with writing love-songs in their
barks.   230

ORLANDO

I pray you mar no moe[156] of my verses with reading them ill-
favouredly.

JAQUES

Rosalind is your love's name?

ORLANDO

Yes, just.[157]

JAQUES

I do not like her name.   235

ORLANDO

There was no thought of pleasing you when she was christened.

JAQUES

What stature[158] is she of?

ORLANDO

Just as high as my heart.[159]

JAQUES

You are full of pretty answers. Have you not been acquainted
with goldsmiths' wives,[160] and conned[161] them out of rings?   240

ORLANDO

Not so; but I answer you right painted cloth,[162] from whence[163]
you have studied your questions.

JAQUES

You have a nimble wit;[164] I think 't was made of Atalanta's
heels.[165] Will you sit down with me, and we two will rail against
our mistress[166] the world, and all our misery?   245

167 *chide no breather but* – "blame no one who breathes (i.e. no living person) except".

168 *change* – "exchange".

169 *By my troth* – "Indeed". Jaques is also tired of Orlando. He says that he was looking for a fool (Touchstone) when he found Orlando, suggesting insultingly that he found in Orlando a fool.

170 *He* – "The fool you are seeking".

171 *look but in* – "only look into (the brook)".

172 *mine own figure* – "my own face". In the next speech, Orlando plays with two meanings of *figure*: Jaques, he says, will see either the figure (= face) of a fool or the figure (= number) O *(cipher)*. – Jaques, he suggests, is either a fool or a person of no importance (a cipher).

173 *tarry* – "stay".

174 *Signior Love* – said in mockery of Orlando as a lover. *Signior:* an old spelling of the Italian word for "Master" or "Mister". In reply, Orlando uses the corresponding French title, *Monsieur*.

175 *adieu:* "good-bye" (French).

176 *a saucy . . . with him* – "a rude manservant, and under that pretence (*habit* – literally, "clothes") trick him."

ORLANDO

I will chide no breather[167] in the world but myself, against whom
I know most faults.

JAQUES

The worst fault you have is to be in love.

ORLANDO

'T is a fault I will not change[168] for your best virtue. I am weary
of you.   250

JAQUES

By my troth,[169] I was seeking for a fool when I found you.

ORLANDO

He[170] is drowned in the brook: look but[171] in, and you shall see
him.

JAQUES

There I shall see mine own figure.[172]

ORLANDO

Which I take to be either a fool or a cipher.   255

JAQUES

I 'll tarry[173] no longer with you: farewell, good Signior Love.[174]

ORLANDO

I am glad of your departure: adieu,[175] good Monsieur Melancholy.   [*Exit* JAQUES

ROSALIND

[*To* CELIA] I will speak to him like a saucy lackey,[176] and under
that habit play the knave with him. [*Calling*] Do you hear, 260
forester?

127

177 *would you* – "do you want".

178 *what is 't o'clock* – "what time is it" (*o'clock* – "by the clock").

179 *detect . . . Time* – "show the slow movement of time" (personified). Orlando's regular sighs and groans will count minutes and hours like the hands of a clock.

180 *proper* – "suitable (as an expression)". The sayings about time seem to show contrasts in nearly all languages. Time is seen as travelling fast or slowly according to circumstances, and Orlando and Rosalind play with this idea.

181 *in divers paces* – "at different *(divers)* speeds". The word *paces* continues the image of the foot for the movement of time. The next two lines refer particularly to the different speeds at which a horse moves. *ambles*, walks without hurry. *trots*, runs. *gallops*, runs at top speed.

182 *trots hard* – "goes at an uncomfortable, uneven trot".

183 *between the contract . . . solemnized* – "between the time of the agreement to marry and the day of the marriage ceremony (*solemnized*, officially and publicly completed)".

184 *if the interim . . . se'nnight* – "even if the period in between is only a week (*se'nnight*, seven nights)".

185 *hard* – "uncomfortable".

ORLANDO

Very well: what would you?[177]

ROSALIND

I pray you, what is 't o'clock?[178]

ORLANDO

You should ask me, what time o' day: there 's no clock in the
forest. 265

ROSALIND

Then there is no true lover in the forest; else sighing every
minute and groaning every hour would detect[179] the lazy foot
of Time as well as a clock.

ORLANDO

And why not the swift foot of Time? Had not that been as
proper?[180] 270

ROSALIND

By no means, sir. Time travels in divers[181] paces with divers
persons. I 'll tell you who Time ambles withal, who Time trots
withal, who Time gallops withal, and who he stands still withal.

ORLANDO

I prithee, who doth he trot withal?

ROSALIND

Marry, he trots hard[182] with a young maid between the con- 275
tract[183] of her marriage and the day it is solemnized: if the
interim[184] be but a se'nnight, Time's pace is so hard[185] that it
seems the length of seven year.

ORLANDO

Who ambles Time withal?

129

186 *lacks Latin* – "cannot understand Latin". Good priests were expected to know Latin, the language of religious studies. A priest ignorant of Latin does not study and has more time for sleep.

187 *the one*, i.e. the ignorant priest, by contrast with *the other*, the rich man.

188 *the burden . . . learning* – "the load (on the mind) of study, which makes a man lean and wastes his strength".

189 *go as softly* – "walks as slowly".

190 *in the vacation:* Law courts, like schools and universities, have *terms*, and, between them, *vacations.*

191 *pretty youth:* Orlando finds the "young man" *(youth)* very pleasant *(pretty).*

192 *in the skirts . . . fringe upon* – "on the edge of the forest as if our house were attached to it like the ornamental border *(fringe)* sewn on".

193 *native of* – "a person who was born in".

194 *As the cony . . . kindled* – "(yes) just like the rabbit *(cony)* that one sees living in the place where it was born *(kindled)*".

195 *Your accent . . . dwelling* – "Your way of speaking is rather more refined than you would acquire in a place so far away (from the court and educated people)".

ROSALIND

With a priest that lacks Latin[186] and a rich man that hath not the 280
gout; for the one[187] sleeps easily because he cannot study, and
the other lives merrily because he feels no pain; the one lacking
the burden of lean[188] and wasteful learning, the other knowing
no burden of heavy tedious penury: these Time ambles withal.

ORLANDO

Who doth he gallop withal?   285

ROSALIND

With a thief to the gallows; for though he go as softly[189] as foot
can fall, he thinks himself too soon there.

ORLANDO

Who stays it still withal?

ROSALIND

With lawyers in the vacation;[190] for they sleep between term
and term, and then they perceive not how Time moves.   290

ORLANDO

Where dwell you, pretty youth?[191]

ROSALIND

With this shepherdess, my sister; here in the skirts[192] of the
forest, like fringe upon a petticoat.

ORLANDO

Are you native[193] of this place?

ROSALIND

As the cony,[194] that you see dwell where she is kindled.   295

ORLANDO

Your accent is something finer[195] than you could purchase in
so removed a dwelling.

196 *of many* – "by a lot of people".

197 *religious* – "devoted to the religious life of prayer and study in a lonely place (i.e. as a hermit)". Rosalind invents this "uncle" to explain her refined accent and her knowledge of the world.

198 See p. 90, note 65.

199 *courtship:* Rosalind plays with two meanings: (i) life at court; (ii) wooing (the usual meaning).

200 *read many lectures* – "give many warnings".

201 *be touched . . . withal* – "affected with so many foolish faults *(giddy offences)* as he has generally accused *(taxed)* all women of having".

202 *evils . . . women* – "faults that he declared women to be guilty of".

203 *I will not . . . sick* – "I will give my medicine *(physic)* only to those who are ill" (i.e. those who are in love).

204 *a man haunts . . . with carving* – "a man frequently in the forest who harms our young trees by carving the name".

205 *forsooth* – "indeed" (said with scorn).

206 *deifying* – "treating as if it belonged to a goddess".

207 *fancy-monger* – "dealer in love" (compare fishmonger, ironmonger, etc.)

208 *quotidian* – "fever which comes back every day".

209 *love-shaked* – "shaken (through all his body as if with a fever) by love".

210 *my uncle's marks,* i.e. the signs of a man in love that her uncle taught her to look for.

211 *cage of rushes* – "cage made of straw" (i.e. love is a kind of prison from which one can easily escape).

ROSALIND

I have been told so of many:[196] but indeed, an old religious[197]
uncle of mine taught me to speak, who was in his youth an
inland[198] man; one that knew courtship[199] too well, for there he 300
fell in love. I have heard him read many lectures[200] against it, and
I thank God I am not a woman, to be touched[201] with so many
giddy offences as he hath generally taxed their whole sex withal.

ORLANDO

Can you remember any of the principal evils that he laid to the
charge[202] of women?   305

ROSALIND

There were none principal; they were all like one another as
halfpence are; every one fault seeming monstrous till his fellow-
fault came to match it.

ORLANDO

I prithee, recount some of them.

ROSALIND

No, I will not cast away my physic[203] but on those that are sick. 310
There is a man haunts[204] the forest, that abuses our young plants
with carving "Rosalind" on their barks; hangs odes upon haw-
thorns, and elegies on brambles; all, forsooth,[205] deifying[206] the
name of Rosalind. If I could meet that fancy-monger,[207] I would
give him some good counsel, for he seems to have the quotidian[208] 315
of love upon him.

ORLANDO

I am he that is so love-shaked;[209] I pray you, tell me your
remedy.

ROSALIND

There is none of my uncle's marks[210] upon you. He taught me
how to know a man in love; in which cage of rushes[211] I am sure 320
you are not prisoner.

212 *blue eye and sunken* – "eyes with dark circles round them (showing lack of sleep) and looking dull".

213 *an unquestionable spirit* – "an unwillingness to talk".

214 *your having . . . revenue* – "what you possess in the way of a beard is like the wealth *(revenue)* of a younger brother", i.e. there is very little of either.

215 *hose should be ungartered*, i.e. his leg garments, instead of being properly pulled up and firmly tied with a *garter* (a band round the leg for this purpose), should be loose and wrinkled.

216 *bonnet unbanded*, i.e. his hat *(bonnet)*, instead of having the fashionable band tied round it, should be carelessly worn without it.

217 *demonstrating . . . desolation* – "showing outwardly a condition of misery *(desolation)* in which you no longer care about your appearance".

218 *point-device . . . accoutrements, as* – "very correct in your way of dressing, more as if".

219 *You may . . . she does* – "It would be as easy to make the person whom you love believe it, though I am sure she is readier to believe it (that you love her) than to admit that she does". Rosalind is talking about herself.

220 *give the lie . . . consciences* – "deny their secret thoughts".

221 *Neither rhyme nor reason* – "Neither verse nor plain language" (i.e. no form of expression).

ORLANDO

What were his marks?

ROSALIND

A lean cheek, which you have not; a blue eye[212] and sunken,
which you have not; an unquestionable[213] spirit, which you
have not; a beard neglected, which you have not; but I pardon 325
you for that, for simply your having[214] in beard is a younger
brother's revenue. Then, your hose should be ungartered,[215]
your bonnet unbanded,[216] your sleeve unbuttoned, your shoe
untied, and everything about you demonstrating a careless
desolation.[217] But you are no such man; you are rather point- 330
device[218] in your accoutrements, as loving yourself than seeming
the lover of any other.

ORLANDO

Fair youth, I would I could make thee believe I love.

ROSALIND

Me believe it? You may as soon[219] make her that you love
believe it; which, I warrant, she is apter to do than to confess she 335
does; that is one of the points in which women still give the
lie[220] to their consciences. But, in good sooth, are you he that
hangs the verses on the trees, wherein Rosalind is so admired?

ORLANDO

I swear to thee, youth, by the white hand of Rosalind, I am that
he, that unfortunate he. 340

ROSALIND

But are you so much in love as your rhymes speak?

ORLANDO

Neither rhyme nor reason[221] can express how much.

135

222 *merely* – "entirely".

223 *a dark house and a whip* – refers to the way madmen were treated.

224 *they*, i.e. lovers.

225 *profess . . . counsel* – "claim that I can cure it by giving advice" (and not by punishment).

226 *set him* – "gave him the duty".

227 *at which time . . . youth* – "and then (when he came to woo), as a changeable *(moonish)* young person, I used to". (*Moonish*, because changing, as does the moon.)

228 *effeminate* – "girlish in behaviour".

229 *fantastical, apish, shallow* – "full of strange fancies, foolish tricks (like an ape), without deep feelings".

230 *cattle of this colour* – "creatures of this kind".

231 *then entertain . . . forswear him* – "first make him welcome, then break promises to him".

232 *drave . . . madness* – "drove my lover *(suitor)* from the mad state of mind caused by love to a state of real *(living)* madness".

233 *forswear . . . monastic* – "take a vow to give up the way of life followed by most people, and to live in a hidden place *(nook)* entirely as a man who has given himself to the service of God".

234 *take upon me* – "make it my duty".

235 *liver*, the part of the body where it was believed that love and strong passions originated. Rosalind, in offering to *wash* Orlando's liver *clean*, meant to clean the passion of love out of his body.

236 *sound* – "healthy".

237 *would not* – "do not wish to".

238 *but* – "only".

239 *cote* – "cottage".

AUDREY

I do not know what "poetical" is. Is it honest in deed and word?
Is it a true thing?

TOUCHSTONE

No, truly; for the truest poetry[15] is the most feigning; and   15
lovers are given to[16] poetry, and what they swear in poetry may
be said[17] as lovers they do feign.

AUDREY

Do you wish, then,[18] that the gods had made me poetical?

TOUCHSTONE

I do, truly; for thou swearest to me thou art honest: now, if
thou wert a poet, I might have some hope thou didst feign.   20

AUDREY

Would you not have me honest?

TOUCHSTONE

No, truly, unless thou wert hard-favoured;[19] for honesty
coupled[20] to beauty is to have honey[21] a sauce to sugar.

JAQUES

[*Aside*] A material[22] fool!

AUDREY

Well, I am not fair, and therefore I pray the gods make me   25
honest.

TOUCHSTONE

Truly, and to cast away[23] honesty upon a foul slut were to put
good meat into an unclean dish.

AUDREY

I am not a slut, though I thank the gods I am foul.

24 *hereafter* – "later".

25 *be it as it may be* – "in any case"; "anyway".

26 *to that end* – "for that purpose".

27 *Sir Oliver Mar-text:* "Mar-text" suggests one who will destroy *(mar)* the true meaning of the words in the prayer book. Sir Oliver (*Sir* was added to the names of all priests) is one of the false, untrained priests of the time who were willing to perform marriages against the rules of the Church.

28 *couple* – "marry".

29 *fain* – "like to".

30 *stagger . . . attempt* – "hesitate in carrying out this plan".

31 *temple*, i.e. church.

32 *assembly . . . horn-beasts* – "people present (as witnesses) except the deer (with their horns)".

33 *what though* – "what if it be so".

34 *As horns . . . necessary* – "Although horns are unpleasant, they are needed". In this speech Touchstone plays with several ideas connected with horns; here the idea is that it is unpleasant for a man to have horns on his head – an Elizabethan expression meaning that he was tricked by his wife.

35 *knows no end of* – "does not know the extent of" (also in the next line).

36 *the dowry . . . getting* – "something given to him by his wife; he did not earn it" (a wife's deceiving of her husband is compared to the money *(dowry)* given to him when they married; he did not earn it, but it is his).

37 *Even . . . alone* – "Quite true. (Is it true of) poor men only" (i.e. that they are tricked by their wives).

38 *rascal* – "poor, badly shaped deer" (i.e. great and poor men alike may be deceived, just as noble and mean deer all have horns).

39 *walled town*, i.e. a town with walls for defence round it, as many towns had in Shakespeare's time.

40 *bare brow*, i.e. without "horns", and so resembling a village without walls. Touchstone's argument is that it is better to be a deceived husband than to be an unmarried man because the married man is more honoured.

41 *no skill* – "no ability to defend oneself" (like an open village compared to a walled town).

42 *well met* – "welcome" (also line 59).

43 *dispatch us* – "deal with us" (i.e. marry – the word *dispatch* suggests work done in a hurry).

44 *give:* At a marriage it is usual for the father to "give" his daughter away to the husband.

TOUCHSTONE

Well, praised be the gods for thy foulness! Sluttishness may   30
come hereafter.[24] But be it as[25] it may be, I will marry thee; and
to that end[26] I have been with Sir Oliver Mar-text,[27] the vicar of
the next village, who hath promised to meet me in this place
of the forest and to couple[28] us.

JAQUES

[*Aside*] I would fain[29] see this meeting.   35

AUDREY

Well, the gods give us joy!

TOUCHSTONE

Amen. A man may, if he were of a fearful heart, stagger[30] in
this attempt; for here we have no temple[31] but the wood, no
assembly[32] but horn-beasts. But what though?[33] Courage! As
horns are odious,[34] they are necessary. It is said, "Many a man   40
knows no end[35] of his goods." Right: many a man has good
horns, and knows no end of them. Well, that is the dowry[36] of
his wife; 't is none of his own getting. Horns? Even so.[37] Poor
men alone? No, no; the noblest deer hath them as huge as the
rascal.[38] Is the single man therefore blessed? No, as a walled[39]   45
town is more worthier than a village, so is the forehead of a
married man more honourable than the bare brow[40] of a
bachelor; and by how much defence is better than no skill,[41]
by so much is a horn more precious than to want.

Enter SIR OLIVER MAR-TEXT

Here comes Sir Oliver. Sir Oliver Mar-text, you are well met.[42]   50
Will you dispatch[43] us here under this tree, or shall we go with
you to your chapel?

OLIVER MAR-TEXT

Is there none here to give[44] the woman?

143

45 *on gift of* – "as a present from".

46 *Good even* – "Good evening".

47 *What-ye-call 't* – "Whatever your name is". Touchstone does not know (or pretends not to know) Jaques's name.

48 *God 'ild . . . company* – "thank you for your recent company" (*'ild*, for *yield* – "reward").

49 *Even a toy in hand*, i.e. there is a small matter *(toy)* to be dealt with.

50 *pray be covered* – "please put your hat on again". Touchstone is playing the great courtier and all through this speech he treats the real courtier, Jaques, as if he were a less important man. Jaques took off his hat, not out of respect for Touchstone and Audrey, but because it was correct to stand bare-headed for a church service.

51 *motley*, i.e. fool.

52 *As the ox . . . desires* (line 64), i.e. each man is bound by his desires, just as the ox is by its *bow* (curved wooden piece fitted over the ox's neck when ploughing), the horse by its *curb* (strap used to control a horse by pulling at the lower jaw), and the *falcon* (hawk trained to hunt other birds) by the bells its owner ties to its legs.

53 *as pigeons bill . . . nibbling* – "as *pigeons* (doves) rub beaks together, so people are impatient before marriage *(wedlock)*" (*nibbling*, taking small bites of food).

54 *of your breeding* – "of a noble family like yourself". Jaques accepts Touchstone's pretence of being a courtier although he knows it is false.

55 *under a bush*, i.e. in the open air (without going to church).

56 *will but join . . . wainscot*, i.e. will make very rough work of marrying you, like the rough work done in joining square pieces of board on the walls of a room to make a *wainscot*. The image of rough joining of wooden boards *(panels)* continues: if one panel is made of *timber* (wood for building) which has not been properly dried (and is therefore *green*), that the panel will become smaller *(shrink)* and lose its shape *(warp)*. Then the wainscot will break up, just as a roughly made marriage will break up.

57 *I am not . . . another* – "I believe that I would do better being married by Sir Oliver Mar-text than being married by another priest".

58 *like* – "likely".

59 *well*, i.e. according to the law.

60 *hereafter* – "later on".

the falcon her bells

TOUCHSTONE

I will not take her on gift[45] of any man.

OLIVER MAR–TEXT

Truly, she must be given, or the marriage is not lawful.   55

JAQUES

[*Coming forward, taking off his hat*] Proceed, proceed; I 'll give her.

TOUCHSTONE

Good even,[46] good Master What-ye-call 't.[47] How do you, sir? You are very well met: God 'ild you[48] for your last company; I am very glad to see you. Even a toy[49] in hand here, sir. Nay,   60 pray be covered.[50]

JAQUES

Will you be married, motley?[51]

TOUCHSTONE

As the ox hath his bow,[52] sir, the horse his curb, and the falcon her bells, so man hath his desires; and as pigeons bill,[53] so wedlock would be nibbling.   65

JAQUES

And will you, being a man of your breeding,[54] be married under a bush[55] like a beggar? Get you to church, and have a good priest that can tell you what marriage is: this fellow will but join you together as they join wainscot;[56] then one of you will prove a shrunk panel, and like green timber, warp, warp.   70

TOUCHSTONE

[*Aside*] I am not in the mind[57] but I were better to be married of him than of another; for he is not like[58] to marry me well;[59] and not being well married, it will be a good excuse for me hereafter[60] to leave my wife.

145

61 *must be married*, i.e. properly in a church.

62 *must . . . bawdry* – "shall (otherwise) be immoral." Lines 79–81 and 82–4 are from an old song, now lost; Touchstone may have changed some words to suit the occasion.

63 *Wind* – "Turn".

64 *Ne'er . . . calling* – "Not one of these strange bad fellows shall make me give up my way of life (*calling*, i.e. as a false priest)".

(III.iv) Rosalind talks to Celia about her love, complaining that Orlando has not kept his appointment. Celia warns her that Orlando may be a false lover.

1 *Never* – "Do not".

2 *become* – "suit" (Rosalind is still dressed as Ganymede).

JAQUES

Go thou with me, and let me counsel thee.   75

TOUCHSTONE

Come, sweet Audrey:
We must be married,[61] or we must live in bawdry.[62]
Farewell, good Master Oliver: not

     O sweet Oliver,
     O brave Oliver,   80
  Leave me not behind thee;

but

     Wind[63] away,
     Be gone, I say;
  I will not to wedding with thee.
        [*Exeunt* JAQUES, TOUCHSTONE *and* AUDREY

OLIVER MAR-TEXT

'T is no matter. Ne'er a fantastical[64] knave of them all shall   85
flout me out of my calling.   [*Exit*

Scene IV. *The forest.*
Enter ROSALIND *and* CELIA.

ROSALIND

Never[1] talk to me; I will weep.

CELIA

Do, I prithee; but yet have the grace to consider that tears do not
become[2] a man.

ROSALIND

But have I not cause to weep?

CELIA

As good cause as one would desire; therefore weep.   5

3 *the dissembling colour* – "the colour of deceiving". It was believed that the colour of the hair showed a person's character. In particular, people with red hair had the reputation of being deceivers, probably because of an old belief that *Judas*, who betrayed Jesus to his enemies with a *kiss*, had red hair.

4 *browner*, i.e. not quite so red. The Elizabethans often used the word "brown" to describe red hair.

5 *Judas's own children*, i.e. very like the kisses of Judas, intended to deceive.

6 *I' faith* – "Indeed".

7 *your chestnut . . . only colour* – "*chestnut* (reddish-brown, the colour of a kind of nut), as you know, was always the only good colour".

8 *holy bread* – "bread blessed in church and then given to the poor".

9 *hath bought . . . Diana* – "has obtained a pair of lips that once belonged to Diana (the virgin goddess of the Romans)", i.e. very pure, passionless lips.

10 *winter's sisterhood*, i.e. the most cold and pure order (the image is of a society of women devoted to purity).

11 *pick-purse*, thief who steals purses containing money.

12 *for his verity* – "as for his truthfulness".

13 *concave . . . goblet* – "hollow (i.e. without truth in him) as a wine-cup *(goblet)* with its ornamental cover on it (showing that it was empty)".

a covered goblet

148

ROSALIND

His very hair is of the dissembling[3] colour.

CELIA

Something browner[4] than Judas's. Marry, his kisses are Judas's own children.[5]

ROSALIND

faith,[6] his hair is of a good colour.

CELIA

An excellent colour: your chestnut[7] was ever the only colour.　10

ROSALIND

And his kissing is as full of sanctity as the touch of holy bread.[8]

CELIA

He hath bought[9] a pair of cast lips of Diana: a nun of winter's sisterhood[10] kisses not more religiously; the very ice of chastity is in them.

ROSALIND

But why did he swear he would come this morning, and comes　15
not?

CELIA

Nay, certainly there is no truth in him.

ROSALIND

Do you think so?

CELIA

Yes; I think he is not a pick-purse[11] nor a horse-stealer; but for
his verity[12] in love, I do think him as concave[13] as a covered　20
goblet or a worm-eaten nut.

14 *in*, i.e. in love.

15 *tapster . . . reckonings* – A tapster was an inn servant who sold drinks. Celia means that lovers swear to lies like tapsters who declare firmly that false accounts *(reckonings)* are correct.

16 *attends (on)* – "serves".

17 *question* – "talk".

18 *of what parentage I was* – "who my parents were" (the Duke would be interested in the social class of this well-spoken young "man").

19 *brave* – "fine". (Celia's repeated use of *brave* is ironical, like Antony's use of "honourable" for Brutus in Shakespeare's *Julius Caesar*.)

20 *breaks them . . . noble goose:* Celia's statement that Orlando breaks his promises is strengthened by an image from the old sport of tilting – trying to make another horseman fall by riding at him with a lance (a long *staff*). The idea was to ride straight at the other man and strike his shield in the middle; the lance then split from end to end. An inexperienced *(puisny)* tilter, who spurred his horse in such a way as to cause it to turn sideways, made his lance break across *(traverse)*, and this was a disgrace; the man made himself look a fool *(goose)*. Celia says that Orlando breaks his promises in this way, and deals a crooked *(athwart)* blow to his lady's heart.

21 *all 's brave . . . guides* – "all is considered fine when a young man is responsible for it (*mounts* – literally 'rides the horse') and his folly is the leader".

22 *of love*, i.e. of his sorrows in love.

the shepherd that complained of love[22]

150

ROSALIND

Not true in love?

CELIA

Yes, when he is in,[14] but I think he is not in.

ROSALIND

You have heard him swear downright he was.

CELIA

"Was" is not "is". Besides, the oath of a lover is no stronger   25
than the word of a tapster;[15] they are both the confirmer of
false reckonings. He attends[16] here in the forest on the Duke
your father.

ROSALIND

I met the Duke yesterday and had much question[17] with him:
he asked me of what parentage[18] I was: I told him, of as good as   30
he; so he laughed and let me go. But what talk we of fathers
when there is such a man as Orlando?

CELIA

O, that's a brave[19] man! He writes brave verses, speaks brave
words, swears brave oaths and breaks them bravely,[20] quite
traverse, athwart the heart of his lover; as a puisny tilter, that   35
spurs his horse but on one side, breaks his staff like a noble goose;
but all 's brave[21] that youth mounts and folly guides. Who
comes here?

Enter CORIN

CORIN

Mistress and master, you have oft enquired
After the shepherd that complained of love,[22]
Who you saw sitting by me on the turf,   40
Praising the proud disdainful shepherdess
That was his mistress.

151

23 *pageant* – "scene". Corin invites them to see, as if it were a play, a a meeting between Silvius (a *true* lover with a *pale* face or complexion) and Phebe (a *scornful*, *proud* mistress, whose cheeks show a *red glow* of annoyance), but he speaks as if the feelings were themselves the actors. In the old "morality plays" actors did represent feelings as if they were characters.

24 *will mark* – "would like to watch".
25 *remove* – "move away".
26 *feedeth* – "gives pleasure to".
27 *I'll prove . . . play* – "I shall play an important part in their affairs".

(III.v) Rosalind and Celia watch Silvius begging Phebe to love him. Phebe is proud and scornful. Rosalind, as "Ganymede", tells her that Silvius is too good for her, and that she should be grateful for his love. The only result is that Phebe falls in love with the disguised Rosalind.

1 *The common . . . pardon* (line 6) – "Even the public *executioner* (man paid to put people to death as a punishment), whose heart is hardened because he is used to the sight of death, asks the condemned man to forgive him *(begs pardon)* before he brings the axe down on the neck bowed *(humbled)* to receive it".

2 *dies . . . drops* – "earns his living by spilling blood".
3 *I fly . . . would not* – "I avoid you because I do not want to".
4 *there is . . . mine eye* – "that my looks are cruel enough to kill".

CELIA

Well, and what of him?

CORIN

If you will see a pageant[23] truly played
Between the pale complexion of true love   45
And the red glow of scorn and proud disdain,
Go hence a little, and I shall conduct you,
If you will mark[24] it.

ROSALIND

O, come, let us remove:[25]
The sight of lovers feedeth[26] those in love.
Bring us to this sight, and you shall say   50
I 'll prove a busy actor[27] in their play.

[*Exeunt*

Scene V. The forest.
Enter PHEBE *followed by* SILVIUS.

SILVIUS

Sweet Phebe, do not scorn me; do not, Phebe!
Say that you love me not, but say not so
In bitterness. The common executioner,[1]
Whose heart the accustomed sight of death makes hard,
Falls not the axe upon the humbled neck   5
But first begs pardon: will you sterner be
Than he that dies and lives[2] by bloody drops?

Enter ROSALIND, CELIA, *and* CORIN *behind*

PHEBE

I would not be thy executioner;
I fly[3] thee, for I would not injure thee.
Thou tell'st me there is murder[4] in mine eye: 10

153

5 *pretty, sure* – "certainly *(sure)* a fine thing to say" (irony).

6 *Who shut . . . atomies* – "which close their gates like cowards (i.e. close their eyelids in fear) against tiny bits of dust *(atomies)*". Phebe argues that it is nonsense for Silvius to say that her eyes (her cruel looks) are killing him (like *tyrants, butchers, murderers*).

7 *with all my heart*, i.e. and really mean it.

8 *counterfeit to swoon* – "pretend to faint". (Now that I am really angry, she tells Silvius, you can pretend that my cruel looks make you faint.)

9 *why*, i.e. "yes".

10 *for shame* – "you should be ashamed".

11 *lean upon . . . moment keeps*, i.e. if Silvius puts his hand on a straw *(rush)* and leans his weight on it, there will be a mark *(cicatrice)* and a clear line where it has pressed *(capable impressure)* on the palm of his hand for a moment or two. Phebe's angry looks make no mark and do not hurt him.

12 *as that . . . near* – "and the time I call 'ever' may be quite soon".

13 *You meet . . . fancy* – "you feel the power of love *(fancy)* as the result of meeting some new person" *(cheek*, for "face").

14 *love's keen arrows* – "the sharp arrows of love". The arrow image goes back to ancient times, when it was believed that Cupid, the god of love, sent unseen arrows from the eyes of one person into the heart of another.

15 *Afflict me* – "make me suffer".

16 *Who might be . . . the wretched* – "Was your mother such a great lady that you have the right to insult this unhappy man and enjoy your triumph *(exult)* over him, both at the same time".

17 *you have no beauty:* We should expect the question to be, "Even if you *are* beautiful . . . must you be proud and without pity?" But Rosalind is speaking to hurt: she cannot see such unusual beauty in Phebe as would shine in the dark and so let Phebe go to bed without a candle to light the way to her room.

'T is pretty,[5] sure, and very probable
That eyes, that are the frail'st and softest things,
Who shut their coward gates[6] on atomies,
Should be called tyrants, butchers, murderers!
Now I do frown on thee with all my heart,[7]   15
And if mine eyes can wound, now let them kill thee:
Now counterfeit[8] to swoon; why,[9] now fall down;
Or if thou canst not, O, for shame,[10] for shame,
Lie not, to say mine eyes are murderers!
Now show the wound mind eye hath made in thee: 20
Scratch thee but with a pin, and there remains
Some scar of it; lean upon a rush,[11]
The cicatrice and capable impressure
Thy palm some moment keeps; but now mine eyes,
Which I have darted at thee, hurt thee not,   25
Nor, I am sure, there is no force in eyes
That can do hurt.

SILVIUS

                O dear Phebe,
If ever – as that "ever"[12] may be near –
You meet in some fresh cheek[13] the power of fancy,
Then shall you know the wounds invisible   30
That love's keen arrows[14] make.

PHEBE

                    But till that time
Come thou not near me; and when that time comes,
Afflict[15] me with thy mocks, pity me not;
As till that time I shall not pity thee.

ROSALIND

[*Coming forward*] And why, I pray you? Who might be[16]
    your mother,   35
That you insult, exult, and all at once,
Over the wretched? What though you have no beauty –[17]

155

18 *Why do you look on me* – "Why are you staring at me like that". (No "man" has ever spoken like this to Phebe before. Phebe is staring at Ganymede with amazement.)

19 *ordinary . . . sale-work* – "common things that nature makes in large numbers for quick sale". (Nature produces large numbers of girls just attractive enough to find husbands; Phebe is this kind of *sale-work*, not one of Nature's special, carefully made articles of beauty.)

20 *'Od's . . . life*, an exclamation, rather like "goodness me". (*'Od* is a form of *God*, but the whole expression has little meaning.)

21 *tangle* – "trap".

22 *faith* – "indeed".

23 *hope not after it* – "do not hope for that (i.e. to win me as a lover)".

24 *'T is not . . . worship* – "in spite of your very dark (*inky*, like ink) eyebrows, your black silky hair, your dark eyes with the gleam of black beads (*bugle*), and your cheeks as smooth as cream and cream-coloured, you will not be able to make me your humble worshipper".

25 *like foggy . . . rain*, i.e. full of sighs (sad deep breaths) and tears, like the wind that blows from the south-west and brings thick clouds (*foggy*) and wind and rain to England.

26 *properer* – "mere good-looking".

27 *That makes . . . children*, i.e. who by marrying plain-looking women fill the world with ugly (*ill-favoured*) children who look like their mothers.

28 *'T is not . . . show her* – "Her mirror does not flatter her; you do, and it is through your eyes (*out of you*) that she sees herself as more good-looking (*proper*) than (the reflection of) any parts of her face (*lineaments*) can make her appear".

29 *know yourself* – "(you must) know your true character".

30 *down on . . . fasting* – "you should kneel down (as is proper when praying to God) and give thanks to God, taking no food (*fasting*)". Fasting was a sign of sorrow for one's faults, as kneeling was a sign that one was humble before God.

31 *friendly in your ear* – "as friendly advice, not to be heard by anyone else".

32 *Sell . . . all markets*, i.e. marry while you have the chance; you may not find another man who will want you as his wife. The image is of selling goods at a reasonable price instead of waiting for a better price and running the risk of not selling at all.

33 *Cry . . . mercy* – "Beg the man (Silvius) to forgive you".

34 *Foul is most . . . scoffer* – "if a person is ugly (*being foul*), the ugliest way to behave is to be proud and scornful (a *scoffer*)".

35 *chide a year together* – "scold (me) for a year without stopping".

36 *He's fallen . . . foulness:* Rosalind speaks first to Phebe, on one side of her, and then to Silvius, on the other. (*foulness* here means "bad behaviour").

37 *sauce* – "scold sharply" (like the sharp taste of sauce).

As, by my faith, I see no more in you
Than without candle may go dark to bed –
Must you be therefore proud and pitiless?   40
Why, what means this? Why do you look[18] on me?
I see no more in you than in the ordinary[19]
Of nature's sale-work. 'Od 's[20] my little life,
I think she means to tangle[21] my eyes too!
No, faith,[22] proud mistress, hope not after[23] it;   45
'T is not your inky[24] brows, your black silk hair,
Your bugle eyeballs, nor your cheek of cream,
That can entame my spirits to your worship.
You foolish shepherd, wherefore do you follow her,
Like foggy south,[25] puffing with wind and rain?   50
You are a thousand times a properer[26] man
Than she a woman. 'T is such fools as you
That makes the world full of ill-favoured children.[27]
'T is not her glass,[28] but you, that flatters her;
And out of you she sees herself more proper   55
Than any of her lineaments can show her.
But mistress, know yourself:[29] down on your knees,[30]
And thank heaven, fasting, for a good man's love;
For I must tell you friendly in your ear,[31]
Sell when you can; you are not for all markets.[32]   60
Cry the man mercy;[33] love him, take his offer;
Foul is most foul,[34] being foul to be a scoffer.
So take her to thee, shepherd: fare you well.

PHEBE

Sweet youth, I pray you chide a year together;[35]
I had rather hear you chide than this man woo.   65

ROSALIND

[*To* PHEBE] He 's fallen in love with your foulness,[36] [*To*
SILVIUS] and she 'll fall in love with my anger. If it be so, as
fast as she answers thee with frowning looks. I 'll sauce[37] her with
bitter words. [*To* PHEBE] Why look you so upon me?

38 *For no ill will . . . you* – "(Certainly) not because I wish to harm you".

39 *falser . . . wine* – "less to be trusted than solemn promises made by a man who has taken too much wine (when promises are readily made but quickly forgotten)". (Of those present, only Celia knows how "false" Ganymede is.)

40 *will know . . . hard by* – "want to know where I live, my home is at the group of olive trees quite near here".

41 *ply her hard* – "do not stop wooing her".

42 *look on him* – "respect him".

43 *though all . . . sight as he* – "even if every man in the world could look at you, no other man could be so deceived by his eyes *(abused in sight)* (into thinking you beautiful)".

44 *Dead shepherd . . . first sight:* Line 81 was written by Christopher Marlowe (see p. 138, note 13) in his poem, *Hero and Leander*, first printed in 1598. In pastoral poetry (see Introduction, p. xix) poets were often described as "shepherds", and here the *dead shepherd* is Marlowe himself. (*thy saw of might* – "how powerfully right your saying was").

45 *Wherever . . . would be,* i.e. anyone who is really sorry would try to help.

46 *By giving . . . extermined* – "by giving me your love, you will put an end to both your sorrow and my grief" (because that will make Silvius happy and so remove the need for Phebe's pity).

PHEBE

For no ill will[38] I bear you. 70

ROSALIND

I pray you, do not fall in love with me,
For I am falser than vows made in wine;[39]
Besides, I like you not. If you will know[40] my house,
'T is at the tuft of olives, here hard by.
Will you go, sister? [*To* SILVIUS] Shepherd, ply[41] her hard. 75
Come, sister. [*To* PHEBE] Shepherdess, look on him better,[42]
And be not proud: though all the world[43] could see,
None could be so abused in sight as he.
Come, to our flock.

[*Exeunt* ROSALIND, CELIA *and* CORIN

PHEBE

[*To herself*] Dead shepherd,[44] now I find thy saw of might, 80
"Who ever loved that loved not at first sight?"

SILVIUS

Sweet Phebe –

PHEBE

Ha, what sayest thou, Silvius?

SILVIUS

Sweet Phebe, pity me.

PHEBE

Why, I am sorry for thee, gentle Silvius. 85

SILVIUS

Wherever sorrow is, relief would be.[45]
If you do sorrow at my grief in love,
By giving love,[46] your sorrow and my grief
Were both extermined.

47 *Thou hast . . . neighbourly:* The Bible instruction to "love thy neighbour" (*Leviticus* 19:18) means to love one's fellow-men. In this sense Phebe says she loves Silvius. But Silvius does not want *neighbourly* love; he wants the love of a woman for a man, which is of a different kind. Phebe is making fun of him.

48 *were covetousness* – "would be wanting someone else's possessions" (which was forbidden in the Bible – *Exodus* 20:17).

49 *not that I bear . . . endure:* "not because I love you, but because *(since that)* you are so good at talking about love, that I will bear your company, which was annoyingly tiring *(irksome)* to me before *(erst)*". Phebe makes a show of friendship towards Silvius because she hopes to make use of him as a messenger to "Ganymede".

50 *employ thee* – "give you a job to do for me".

51 *in such . . . grace* – "in such need of heaven's favour" (because his "goddess" Phebe, has given him so little favour).

52 *most plenteous . . . smile:* The image is of the very poor man who, according to the Bible, had permission to collect *(glean)* any grain *(ears* of corn) dropped or missed by the reapers at harvest time. If the harvesters are kind, they will *scatter* some broken ears of corn for the gleaner. Silvius will find a few smiles scattered by Phebe a very rich *(most plenteous)* crop, even if someone else has most of her love *(the main harvest)*.

53 *erewhile* – "a short time ago".

54 *bounds* – "ground marked off as belonging to it".

55 *carlot* – "peasant" (i.e. the man described in II.iv.74–8).

56 *peevish* – "foolish".

57 *do well* – "are pleasant".

58 *becomes* – "suits".

160

PHEBE

Thou hast my love; is not that neighbourly?[47]   90

SILVIUS

I would have you.

PHEBE

         Why, that were covetousness.[48]
Silvius, the time was that I hated thee,
And yet it is not that I bear[49] thee love;
But since that thou canst talk of love so well,
Thy company, which erst was irksome to me,   95
I will endure, and I 'll employ thee[50] too;
But do not look for further recompense
Than thine own gladness that thou are employed.

SILVIUS

So holy and so perfect is my love, .
And I in such a poverty of grace,[51]   100
That I shall think it a most plenteous crop[52]
To glean the broken ears after the man
That the main harvest reaps: loose now and then
A scattered smile, and that I 'll live upon.

PHEBE

Know'st thou the youth that spoke to me erewhile?[53]   105

SILVIUS

Not very well, but I have met him oft;
And he hath bought the cottage and the bounds[54]
That the old carlot[55] once was master of.

PHEBE

Think not I love him, though I ask for him;
'T is but a peevish[56] boy; yet he talks well;   110
But what care I for words? Yet words do well,[57]

161

59 *make a proper man* – "grow up to become a very good-looking man".

60 *faster . . . heal it up*, i.e. what he said hurt my feelings, but the beauty of his eyes immediately stopped the pain.

61 *for his years* – "for a boy of his age".

62 *His leg . . . 't is well:* The shape of an Elizabethan man's legs was important. Phebe says that Ganymede's legs are not particularly well shaped *(but so so)*, but she likes them.

63 *more lusty* – "brighter".

64 *'t was . . . damask*, i.e. the difference (between the colour of his lips and the colour in his cheeks) was just the same as the difference between all-red *(constant red)* roses and roses of mixed red and white *(damask)*.

65 *had they marked . . . parcels* – "if they had observed him part by part".

66 *gone near to fall* – "very nearly fallen".

67 *for my part* – "as for me".

68 *what had he to do* – "what right had he".

69 *am remembered* – "remember it".

70 *answered not again*, i.e. did not give him a sharp answer *(again* – "back").

71 *that's all one* – "that does not matter".

72 *omittance is no quittance* – "omitting (to answer him angrily) does not mean that he has my pardon *(quittance)*".

73 *straight* – "immediately".

74 *matter* – "substance (of the letter)".

75 *passing short* – "extremely *(passing)* short and sharp".

When he that speaks them pleases those that hear.
It is a pretty youth: not very pretty:
But sure, he 's proud: and yet his pride becomes[58] him.
He 'll make[59] a proper man: the best thing in him   115
Is his complexion; and faster than his tongue[60]
Did make offence, his eye did heal it up.
He is not very tall; yet for his years[61] he 's tall:
His leg is but so so;[62] and yet 't is well.
There was a pretty redness in his lip,   120
A little riper and more lusty[63] red
Than that mixed in his cheek; 't was[64] just the difference
Betwixt the constant red, and mingled damask.
There be some women, Silvius, had they marked[65] him
In parcels as I did, would have gone near[66]   125
To fall in love with him; but, for my part,[67]
I love him not nor hate him not; and yet
I have more cause to hate him than to love him;
For what had he to do[68] to chide at me?
He said mine eyes were black and my hair black;   130
And, now I am remembered,[69] scorned at me.
I marvel why I answered not again:[70]
But that 's all one;[71] omittance[72] is no quittance.
I 'll write to him a very taunting letter,
And thou shalt bear it. Wilt thou, Silvius?   135

SILVIUS

Phebe, with all my heart.

PHEBE

I 'll write it straight;[73]
The matter[74] 's in my head and in my heart:
I will be bitter with him and passing short.[75]
Go with me, Silvius.   140

[*Exeunt*

(iv.i) Rosalind makes fun of Jaques's melancholy; experience is useless, she tells him, if it only makes us sad. Orlando arrives late, and receives from Rosalind a "lesson" in love-making. She declares that no man ever died for love. With Celia as witness, Orlando and Rosalind take each other as "husband" and "wife", after which Rosalind warns Orlando of women's changeable ways.

1 *are in extremity of either* - "go to either extreme (of laughter or sadness)".

2 *abominable . . . censure* - "unnatural *(abominable)* fellows, and expose themselves to every ordinary *(modern)* person's blame".

3 *a post*, because a post is heavy (the old meaning of *sad*) and says nothing.

4 *fantastical* - "full of strange imaginings".

5 *politic* - "pretended" (i.e. he pretends to be sad to help him win his case in a law-court).

6 *nice* - "about small, unimportant things".

7 *compounded . . . simples* - "made up of many different qualities" *(simples* - literally, drugs of which a medicine was made up).

8 *the sundry . . . humorous sadness* - "including consideration *(contemplation)* of the various *(sundry)* experiences which I have had in my travels - thinking *(rumination)* often about them produces a very sad state of mind *(humorous sadness)* in me".

ACT IV

Scene I. The forest.
Enter ROSALIND, CELIA *and* JAQUES.

JAQUES

I prithee, pretty youth, let me be better acquainted with thee.

ROSALIND

They say you are a melancholy fellow.

JAQUES

I am so; I do love it better than laughing.

ROSALIND

Those that are in extremity of[1] either are abominable[2] fellows, and betray themselves to every modern censure worse than   5 drunkards.

JAQUES

Why, 't is good to be sad and say nothing.

ROSALIND

Why then, 't is good to be a post.[3]

JAQUES

I have neither the scholar's melancholy, which is emulation; nor the musician's, which is fantastical;[4] nor the courtier's, which   10 is proud; nor the soldier's, which is ambitious; nor the lawyer's, which is politic;[5] nor the lady's, which is nice;[6] nor the lover's, which is all these: but it is a melancholy of mine own, compounded[7] of many simples, extracted from many objects, and indeed the sundry contemplation[8] of my travels, in which my   15 often rumination wraps me in a most humorous sadness.

9 *to travel for it*, i.e. to have all the trouble of making long journeys (but also playing on an old meaning of *travel* = "work hard").

10 *God buy you* – "Good-bye".

11 *blank verse*, lines of verse written in five feet (see p. 114, note 100) without rhyme *(blank)*. Most verse speeches in *As You Like It* are in this form; so is Orlando's greeting, which Jaques mocks in prose, suggesting that because Orlando is a lover he likes to speak in poetry.

12 *lisp* – "speak with a foreign accent". As Jaques walks away, Rosalind continues to talk to him about foreign travel. In this part of her speech Shakespeare made fun of the behaviour of people who had travelled abroad and wanted everyone to know it, imitating foreign ways and speaking scornfully of their own country.

13 *disable all the benefits* – "describe as if without value all the good qualities".

14 *be out of love . . . nativity*, "dislike (the country of) your birth *(nativity)*".

15 *that countenance you are* – "with the face *(countenance)* that is yours" (because it does not look foreign enough).

16 *will scarce . . . gondola* – "shall find it hard to believe that you have been to Venice". Venice, with its art treasurers and fine buildings, was a city of great interest for travellers from northern Europe. Then as now the traveller moved *(swam)* along the waterways that take the place of streets by using a kind of flat-bottomed boat *(gondola)*.

17 *how now* – "hullo".

18 *You a lover?* – i.e. how can I think of you as a lover (when you come late)?

19 *serve me . . . trick* – "play such a trick on me again".

20 *within . . . promise* – "less than an hour later than the time I promised".

a gondola

ROSALIND

A traveller! By my faith, you have great reason to be sad. I
fear you have sold your own lands to see other men's: then to
have seen much, and to have nothing, is to have rich eyes and
poor hands.   20

JAQUES

Yes, I have gained my experience.

Enter ORLANDO

ROSALIND

And your experience makes you sad: I had rather have a fool to
make me merry than experience to make me sad – and to travel[9]
for it too!

ORLANDO

Good day and happiness, dear Rosalind!   25

JAQUES

Nay then, God buy[10] you, an you talk in blank verse.[11]
[*He starts walking away*

ROSALIND

Farewell, Monsieur Traveller. Look you lisp[12] and wear strange
suits, disable[13] all the benefits of your own country, be out of
love with your nativity,[14] and almost chide God for making you
that countenance[15] you are; or I will scarce think[16] you have   30
swam in a gondola.
                                                           [*Exit* JAQUES
Why, how now,[17] Orlando, where have you been all this while?
You a lover?[18] An you serve me such another trick,[19] never
come in my sight more.

ORLANDO

My fair Rosalind, I come within an hour[20] of my promise.   35

21 *break but* – "break his promise by only".

22 *Cupid . . . heart-whole* – "Cupid (the Roman god of love – see p. 154, note 14) has struck his shoulder with an arrow, but Cupid's arrow, I am sure, has not wounded his heart" (i.e. he may be lightly affected by love, but his love is not deep or serious).

23 *had as lief be wooed of* – "would as willingly be wooed by".

24 *carries his house . . . you make,* i.e. the snail's shell is its "house", so it can offer this as a marriage gift *(jointure)*; Orlando, by contrast, can offer nothing.

25 *destiny* – "what fortune intends for him in the future".

26 *horns:* See p. 142, note 34. There is the same word-play here as in III.iii. 41–9.

27 *such as you . . . wives for* – "men (in general) have usually to be grateful *(beholding)* to their wives for".

28 *he comes . . . wife,* i.e. the snail already (before his marriage) wears the horns that fortune gives to a married man, and so he spares his wife from blame *(slander)*.

ROSALIND

Break an hour's promise in love? He that will divide a minute
into a thousand parts, and break but[21] a part of the thousand
part of a minute in the affairs of love, it may be said of him that
Cupid[22] hath clapped him o' the shoulder, but I 'll warrant him
heart-whole.   40

ORLANDO

Pardon me, dear Rosalind.

ROSALIND

Nay, an you be so tardy, come no more in my sight: I had as
lief[23] be wooed of a snail.

ORLANDO

Of a snail?

ROSALIND

Ay, of a snail; for though he comes slowly, he carries his house   45
on his head;[24] a better jointure, I think, than you make a woman.
Besides, he brings his destiny[25] with him.

ORLANDO

What 's that?

ROSALIND

Why, horns,[26] which such as you are fain[27] to be beholding to
your wives for; but he comes armed[28] in his fortune and prevents   50
the slander of his wife.

ORLANDO

Virtue is no horn-maker, and my Rosalind is virtuous.

ROSALIND

And I am your Rosalind.

29 *leer* – "face".
30 *in a holiday humour* – "in a gay mood".
31 *like* – "likely".
32 *very very* – "real".
33 *gravelled . . . matter*, i.e. puzzled as to what to say next.
34 *occasion* – "the opportunity".
35 *are out* – "have nothing more to say".
36 *warn*, for *warrant* – "protect".
37 *cleanliest shift* – "best way of getting out of the difficulty".
38 *denied* – "refused".

39 *puts you . . . new matter* – "makes you beg *(entreat)* for it, and that gives you a new subject to talk about".
40 *out, being before* – "unable to find a subject when he is in the presence of".
41 *that should you* – "*you* would be out".
42 *think my honesty . . . wit* – "think that my virtue *(honesty)* was of a worse kind *(ranker)* than my cleverness (if I kept you)".
43 *of my suit:* Orlando wants to know whether he would be "out of" (unsuccessful in) his wooing.

CELIA

It pleases him to call you so; but he hath a Rosalind of a better leer[29] than you. 55

ROSALIND

Come, woo me, woo me; for now I am in a holiday humour,[30] and like[31] enough to consent. What would you say to me now, an I were your very very[32] Rosalind?

ORLANDO

I would kiss before I spoke.

ROSALIND

Nay, you were better speak first, and when you were gravelled[33] for lack of matter, you might take occasion[34] to kiss. Very good orators, when they are out,[35] they will spit; and for lovers, lacking – God warn[36] us! – matter, the cleanliest shift[37] is to kiss. 60

ORLANDO

How if the kiss be denied?[38] 65

ROSALIND

Then she puts you to entreaty,[39] and there begins new matter.

ORLANDO

Who could be out,[40] being before his beloved mistress?

ROSALIND

Marry, that should you,[41] if I were your mistress, or I should think my honesty ranker[42] than my wit.

ORLANDO

What, of my suit?[43] 70

44 *apparel* – "clothing" with word-play on *suit* as (i) wooing, (ii) clothes.

45 *in her person* – "speaking as if I were she".

46 *die by attorney* – "get someone else to die for you" (*attorney* – "a representative recognised by law").

47 *almost six . . . old:* This was the age of the world as reckoned by the Elizabethans from evidence they claimed to find in the Bible.

48 *in a love cause* – "because of love".

49 *Troilus,* a famous lover, son of the king of Troy. He was killed in battle with the ancient Greeks. Chaucer wrote a poem, and Shakespeare a play, about his unhappy love for Cressida.

50 *dashed* – "beaten".

51 *Leander.* In an ancient Greek story, Leander lived at Abydos on one side of the narrow sea Hellespont dividing Europe from Asia. He loved *Hero,* who lived at *Sestos* on the other side. Leander used to swim to her across the Hellespont, guided by Hero's lamp, but one night on his way across he was drowned in a storm. In her grief, Hero threw herself into the sea. Rosalind's account changes the story to suit her argument that no man ever died for love.

52 *many a fair . . . nun* – "for many happy years, even if Hero had become a nun (a woman who has given up everything in the world for religious reasons)".

53 *taken with the cramp* – "attacked by violent pain and stiffening of the limbs (caused by cold)".

54 *chroniclers* – "historians".

55 *found it,* i.e. decided that the cause of his death was.

56 *right* – "real".

57 *mind* – "opinion".

58 *protest* – "declare".

59 *coming-on disposition* "helpful state of mind".

ROSALIND

Not out of your apparel,[44] and yet out of your suit. Am not I
your Rosalind?

ORLANDO

I take some joy to say you are, because I would be talking of
her.

ROSALIND

Well, in her person,[45] I say I will not have you.   75

ORLANDO

Then, in mine own person, I die.

ROSALIND

No, faith, die by attorney.[46] The poor world is almost six
thousand years old,[47] and in all this time there was not any man
died in his own person, *videlicet*, in a love cause.[48] Troilus[49] had
his brains dashed[50] out with a Grecian club; yet he did what he   80
could to die before, and he is one of the patterns of love.
Leander,[51] he would have lived many a fair year,[52] though Hero
had turned nun, if it had not been for a hot midsummer night;
for, good youth, he went but forth to wash him in the Hellespont, and being taken with[53] the cramp, was drowned; and the   85
foolish chroniclers[54] of that age found[55] it was "Hero of Sestos".
But these are all lies: men have died from time to time, and
worms have eaten them, but not for love.

ORLANDO

I would not have my right[56] Rosalind of this mind;[57] for, I
protest,[58] her frown might kill me.   90

ROSALIND

By this hand, it will not kill a fly. But come, now I will be your
Rosalind in a more coming-on[59] disposition, and ask me what
you will, I will grant it.

65 *but when? Why now*: According to the law in Shakespeare's time, a statement by a man and woman in front of a witness, declaring that they took each other "now" as husband and wife, was a full marriage. Orlando and Rosalind do in fact marry (without Orlando's knowing it) at this point, though the Church required a second, religious marriage later.

66 *fast* – "completely" (the marriage would be complete in law, but not yet complete in the view of the Church).

67 *ask you for your commission*, i.e. ask what right you have to take Rosalind as your wife without her consent. Celia has not yet asked Rosalind whether she will have Orlando as her husband.

68 *goes before the priest*: Rosalind has said "I do take thee, Orlando . . ." before the "priest" (Celia) has asked the question, "Will you, Rosalind . . .?"

69 *runs before* – "goes ahead of".

70 *winged*, i.e. they move as fast as if they had wings.

71 *have* – "keep".

72 *For ever and a day*, a common saying, meaning "for ever and ever".

73 *April*, i.e. as pleasant as a spring month.

74 *December*, i.e. as cold and hard as a winter month.

75 *May*, i.e. as bright and fresh as the beginning of summer.

76 *the sky changes*, i.e. it becomes dull and cold (as winter).

77 *a Barbary cock-pigeon*, the male of a kind of pigeon, often black, originally from North Africa *(Barbary)* and supposed to be very possessive about its female *(hen)* pigeon.

78 *clamorous . . . rain* – "noisily complaining than a *parrot* (brightly coloured talking bird) is before the rain comes".

79 *new-fangled* – "foolishly fond of change".

ORLANDO

I will.

ROSALIND

Ay, but when?[65]

ORLANDO

Why, now, as fast[66] as she can marry us.   110

ROSALIND

Then you must say, "I take thee, Rosalind, for wife."

ORLANDO

I take thee, Rosalind, for wife.

ROSALIND

I might ask you for your commission,[67] but I do take thee,
Orlando, for my husband. There 's a girl goes before[68] the priest;
and certainly a woman's thought runs before[69] her actions.   115

ORLANDO

So do all thoughts; they are winged.[70]

ROSALIND

Now tell me how long you would have[71] her after you have
possessed her.

ORLANDO

For ever and a day.[72]

ROSALIND

Say "a day" without the "ever". No, no, Orlando; men are   120
April[73] when they woo, December[74] when they wed; maids are
May[75] when they are maids, but the sky changes[76] when they
are wives. I will be more jealous of thee than a Barbary[77] cock-
pigeon over his hen, more clamorous[78] than a parrot against rain,
more new-fangled[79] than an ape, more giddy in my desires than   125

80 *like Diana in the fountain:* Many *fountains* (ornamental constructions using flowing water) included a stone figure of the goddess Diana. The water flowing over the face of this figure suggested, as an image, a crying woman.

81 *hyen,* for *hyena,* an animal whose cry sounds like loud laughter.

82 *my Rosalind,* i.e. the real Rosalind.

83 *the wiser, the waywarder* – "the wiser (a woman is), the more inclined she is to do just as she likes".

84 *make the doors . . . casement* – "shut the doors against (i.e. try to stop) a woman's wit (cleverness), and it will go out through the window (casement)". Her "wit" will always find some way out.

85 *Wit, whither wilt* – "Where are you going, wit", a saying commonly addressed to a person who talked too much.

86 *check* – "way of scolding".

87 *wit could wit have* – "clever answer could her clever mind think of".

88 *take her . . . answer* – "catch her without an answer ready"; "find her unable to give you a clever reply".

89 *that woman . . . occasion* – "any woman who cannot show that what she has done wrong is really caused by her husband".

90 *she will breed . . . fool,* i.e. it will grow up to be like her – a fool.

like Diana[80] *in the fountain*

a monkey. I will weep for nothing, like Diana[80] in the fountain, and I will do that when you are disposed to be merry; I will laugh like a hyen,[81] and that when thou art inclined to sleep.

ORLANDO

But will my Rosalind[82] do so?

ROSALIND

By my life, she will do as I do.   130

ORLANDO

O, but she is wise.

ROSALIND

Or else she could not have the wit to do this. The wiser, the waywarder:[83] make the doors[84] upon a woman's wit, and it will out at the casement; shut that, and 't will out at the keyhole; stop that, 't will fly with the smoke out at the chimney.   135

ORLANDO

A man that had a wife with such a wit, he might say, "Wit, whither wilt?"[85]

ROSALIND

Nay, you might keep that check[86] for it till you met your wife's wit going to your neighbour's bed.

ORLANDO

And what wit could wit[87] have to excuse that?   140

ROSALIND

Marry, to say she came to seek you there. You shall never take[88] her without her answer, unless you take her without her tongue. O, that woman that[89] cannot make her fault her husband's occasion, let her never nurse her child herself, for she will breed[90] it like a fool.   145

179

91 *these* – "the next".
92 *go your ways . . . prove* – "go away, then; I know what (kind of man) you would show yourself to be".
93 *but one cast away* – "just one more girl deserted".
94 *By my troth . . . dangerous:* Rosalind wants to make her warning very strong, so she uses a number of small *(pretty)* oaths that it is not dangerously wicked to break *(dangerous)* – "By my faith, most sincerely, may God correct me". There may also be a reference to strong official objections to the use of swear words on the stage.

95 *behind* – "after".
96 *pathetical break-promise* – "miserable breaker of promises".
97 *hollow* – "insincere".
98 *gross . . . unfaithful* – "whole *(gross)* number of unfaithful people (in the world)".
99 *religion* – "faithfulness".
100 *Time is . . . try,* i.e. Time, seen as an old judge *(justice)* who decides such cases, exposes those who make false promises; so Time will judge *(try)* this case (and decide whether Orlando keeps his promise).

that blind, rascally boy

ORLANDO

For these[91] two hours, Rosalind, I will leave thee.

ROSALIND

Alas, dear love, I cannot lack thee two hours!

ORLANDO

I must attend the Duke at dinner; by two o'clock I will be with thee again.

ROSALIND

Ay, go your ways,[92] go your ways; I knew what you would 150
prove. My friends told me as much, and I thought no less. That flattering tongue of yours won me: 't is but one cast away,[93] and so, come death! Two o'clock is your hour?

ORLANDO

Ay, sweet Rosalind.

ROSALIND

By my troth,[94] and in good earnest, and so God mend me, and by 155
all pretty oaths that are not dangerous, if you break one jot of your promise or come one minute behind[95] your hour, I will think you the most pathetical[96] break-promise, and the most hollow[97] lover, and the most unworthy of her you call Rosalind, that may be chosen out of the gross band[96] of the unfaithful; 160
therefore beware my censure, and keep your promise.

ORLANDO

With no less religion[99] than if thou wert indeed my Rosalind; so adieu.

ROSALIND

Well, Time is the old justice[100] that examines all such offenders, and let Time try. Adieu. 165

[*Exit* ORLANDO

101 *simply misused . . . love-prate* – "absolutely disgraced us women in your foolish talk *(prate)* about love" (i.e. how women behave before and after marriage, lines 121–45).

102 *we must have . . . nest*, i.e. Rosalind ought to have her man's clothes pulled off, to show that the person who has given women this terrible reputation is herself a woman. (There is a reference to a very old saying, "It is an ill [= a bad] bird that fouls its own nest", meaning that it is foolish to destroy one's own reputation.)

103 *that* – "I wish that".

104 *affection* – "passion".

105 *the Bay of Portugal*, part of the sea off the coast of Portugal where the water is very deep; sixteenth-century sailors had been unable to find out *(sound)* its depth.

106 *as fast . . . runs out*, i.e. the more passion enters her heart, the more she has to talk about it, and so let it run out (like a pail without a bottom, Celia suggests).

107 *that same . . . be judge* (line 178): Rosalind wants Cupid, the god of love, to judge the depth of her love for Orlando, but she also speaks of him with some annoyance because he causes lovers to suffer. She calls Cupid a *bastard* (born outside marriage), brought into being *(begot)* by sad thought, empty fancy *(spleen)*, and madness; with his eyes covered *(blind)*, the mischievous *(rascally)* boy plays tricks on *(abuses)* everybody's eyes in revenge for his own blindness *(because . . . out)*.

108 *be out of the sight of* – "bear to be away from".

109 *shadow* – "shady place".

(IV.ii) A song in honour of the lord who killed the deer.

CELIA

You have simply misused[101] our sex in your love-prate: we must have your doublet and hose plucked[102] over your head, and show the world what the bird hath done to her own nest.

ROSALIND

O coz, coz, coz, my pretty little coz, that[103] thou didst know how many fathom deep I am in love! But it cannot be sounded: 170 my affection[104] hath an unknown bottom, like the Bay of Portugal.[105]

CELIA

Or rather, bottomless; that as fast as you pour[106] affection in, it runs out.

ROSALIND

No; that same wicked bastard of Venus[107] that was begot of 175 thought, conceived of spleen, and born of madness, that blind rascally boy that abuses everyone's eyes because his own are out, let him be judge how deep I am in love. I 'll tell thee, Aliena, I cannot be out of the sight of[108] Orlando. I 'll go find a shadow,[109] and sigh till he come. 180

CELIA

And I 'll sleep. [*Exeunt*

Scene II. *The forest.*

Enter JAQUES, AMIENS *and Lords, dressed as foresters.*

JAQUES

Which is he that killed the deer?

A LORD

Sir, it was I.

1 *like . . . conqueror*, i.e. as a Roman army commander was presented to the government after his victories.

2 *it would do well to* – "we ought to".

3 *for a branch of victory* – "as a sign of victory". The Roman commander on a victory procession wore a sort of crown made of laurel leaves (a kind of evergreen plant); *branch* also refers to the branch-like shape of the deer's horns.

4 *purpose* – "occasion", i.e. to be sung while the procession forms.

5 *'T is no matter . . . enough*, i.e. it does not matter whether the singing is good, provided that *(so)* there is enough noise. (The actor playing the part of Amiens would be a trained singer, but all the others join in this song. This line serves as an apology for their untrained singing.)

6 *sing him home* – "bring him back with a song".

7 *The rest . . . burden:* This line may be a part of the song, in which case it means that all other men will wear horns in the sense jokingly used in III.iii, or it may be a stage direction accidentally printed in early editions to look like part of the song, in which case it means that the other actors should join in and sing together (as a *burden*, the chorus or part of a song repeated by all) the six lines which follow.

8 *Take thou no scorn* – "Do not be ashamed".

9 *crest* has two meanings: (i) that which grows on the head (horns etc.), (ii) the design used as the special mark of a noble family.

10 *lusty* – "cheerful".

(IV.iii) Again Orlando fails to arrive in time for his appointment. Silvius brings a love-letter in verse which Phebe has given him for the supposed "Ganymede". Rosalind scolds him for loving a woman who so deceives him. Oliver comes to Celia and Rosalind and tells them how Orlando saved him in the forest from a snake and a lioness, as a result of which Orlando himself was wounded. Orlando's kindness has changed Oliver's hatred into love. Rosalind faints on seeing a handkerchief stained with Orlando's blood, and Oliver realises that she is Orlando's lady in disguise.

1 *much Orlando*, i.e. (ironically) there is not much to be seen of Orlando.

2 *I warrant you* – "You can be sure that". (Celia is amusing herself by making fun of Orlando. He has forgotten his appointment, she says, and has gone out, looking like a brave hunter, but intending only to sleep.)

JAQUES

Let 's present him to the Duke, like a Roman conqueror;[1] and it would do well to[2] set the deer's horns upon his head, for a branch of victory.[3] Have you no song, forester, for this purpose?[4]   5

AMIENS

Yes, sir.

JAQUES

Sing it. 'T is no matter[5] how it be in tune, so it make noise enough.

Song

> What shall he have that killed the deer?
> His leather skin and horns to wear: 10
> Then sing him home.[6]
> The rest shall bear this burden.[7]
>
> Take thou no scorn[8] to wear the horn;
> It was a crest[9] ere thou wast born:
> Thy father's father wore it,   15
> And thy father bore it.
> The horn, the horn, the lusty[10] horn,
> Is not a thing to laugh to scorn.

[*Exeunt*

Scene III. *The forest.*
Enter ROSALIND *and* CELIA.

ROSALIND

How say you now, is it not past two o'clock? And here much[1] Orlando!

CELIA

I warrant[2] you, with pure love and troubled brain, he hath ta'en his bow and arrows and is gone forth to – sleep.

3 *stern brow . . . action* – "fierce look and angry movements" (*waspish*, like the *wasp*, a bee-like insect, getting ready to sting).

4 *but . . . messenger* – "only in the position of one carrying a message and not to blame *(guiltless)* for its wording".

5 *Patience . . . swaggerer*, i.e. even the most patient person (*Patience* personified) would be shocked by this letter and would act like someone ready to have a quarrel.

6 *Bear . . . all* – "If one can bear this (insult), one can bear all things".

7 *Were man . . . phoenix*, i.e. even if men were as uncommon as the *phoenix*, an imaginary bird mentioned by the ancient poets; only one phoenix was said to be alive in the world at any time.

8 *'Od 's my will* – "As I wish for (the grace of) God" (an expression of surprise). *'Od* is used for "God" as in III.v.43.

9 *hare . . . hunt*, i.e. "the object that I (Rosalind) am seeking".

10 *Of your own device* – "which you yourself have composed".

11 *turned . . . love* – "fallen into the most extreme form of love".

12 *leàthern* – "rough-skinned" (like leather).

13 *freestone-coloured* – "yellowish brown".

14 *verily* – "truly".

15 *housewife's*, i.e. of a woman who does hard housework.

16 *invent* – "compose".

17 *a man's . . . hand* – "the composition and handwriting of a man".

Enter SILVIUS

Look who comes here.   5

SILVIUS

[*To* ROSALIND] My errand is to you, fair youth.
My gentle Phebe bid me give you this.
                              [*He gives* ROSALIND *a letter*
I know not the contents, but, as I guess
By the stern brow[3] and waspish action
Which she did use as she was writing of it,   10
It bears an angry tenor: pardon me;
I am but as a guiltless[4] messenger.

ROSALIND

[*Reading the letter to herself*] Patience herself would startle[5] at
    this letter
And play the swaggerer. Bear this,[6] bear all!
She says I am not fair, that I lack manners;   15
She calls me proud, and that she could not love me,
Were man[7] as rare as phoenix. 'Od 's my will![8]
Her love is not the hare[9] that I do hunt:
Why writes she so to me? Well, shepherd, well,
This is a letter of your own device.[10]   20

SILVIUS

No, I protest, I know not the contents.
Phebe did write it.

ROSALIND

                 Come, come, you are a fool,
And turned into the extremity[11] of love.
I saw her hand: she has a leathern[12] hand,
A freestone-coloured[13] hand; I verily[14] did think   25
That her old gloves were on, but 't was her hands.
She had a housewife's[15] hand; but that 's no matter.
I say she never did invent[16] this letter;
This is a man's invention,[17] and his hand.

187

18 *Like . . . Christian*, i.e. like someone defying his worst enemy. The expression reflects the frequent wars between Turks (who were Moslems) and Christians in the Middle Ages.

19 *drop forth . . . invention* – "produce such immensely rude composition".

20 *Ethiop . . . countenance* – "terrible words (*Ethiop*, black as an Ethiopian, and so 'threatening'), blacker in their meaning than in their looks" (although the words are written in black ink).

21 *So please you*, i.e. if you wish it.

22 *Phebes me*, i.e. treats me in the way typical of Phebe, with cruelty.

23 *mark* – "note", i.e. listen.

24 *god . . . turned* – "a god who has changed himself into a shepherd" (as happened in some ancient stories).

25 *burned* – "set on fire (with love)".

26 *Why . . . woman's heart* – "Why, having put aside the qualities of a god (in order to take human form), do you make war against (i.e. try to capture) a woman's heart".

27 *Whiles . . . vengeance* – "While ordinary men admired me, that (kind of wooing) could do no harm *(vengeance)*". Rosalind pretends to think that since this suggests that "Ganymede" is not an ordinary man, it means that he is a *beast*. Phebe meant that Ganymede was god-like.

28 *eyne* – "eyes".

29 *Alack . . . aspect* – "oh, what an effect they (Ganymede's eyes) would have on me if they looked kind".

30 *How then . . . move* – "so how very much would I be affected if you made requests *(prayers)*" (instead of scolding).

188

SILVIUS

Sure it is hers.   30

ROSALIND

Why, 't is a boisterous and a cruel style,
A style for challengers: why, she defies me
Like Turk[18] to Christian; women's gentle brain
Could not drop forth[19] such giant-rude invention,
Such Ethiop[20] words, blacker in their effect   35
Than in their countenance. Will you hear the letter?

SILVIUS

So[21] please you, for I never heard it yet;
Yet heard too much of Phebe's cruelty.

ROSALIND

She Phebes[22] me; mark[23] how the tyrant writes.
[*Reads aloud*] "Art thou god,[24] to shepherd turned,   40
          That a maiden's heart hath burned?"[25]
Can a woman rail thus?

SILVIUS

Call you this railing?

ROSALIND

[*Reads*] "Why, thy godhead[26] laid apart,
          War'st thou with a woman's heart?"   45
Did you ever hear such railing?
          "Whiles[27] the eye of man did woo me,
          That could do no vengeance to me."
Meaning me a beast.
          "If the scorn of your bright eyne[28]   50
          Have power to raise such love in mine,
          Alack,[29] in me what strange effect
          Would they work in mild aspect!
          Whiles you chid me, I did love;
          How then[30] might your prayers move!   55

189

31 *love*, i.e. message of love.

32 *by him seal . . . kind* (line 59) – "with him as your messenger *(by him)*, let me know your decision *(mind)* in a closed letter, (saying) whether your youthful nature".

33 *make* – "offer".

34 *study how to die* – "think of the best way to end my life".

35 *What . . . strains upon thee* – "Will you let her use you like a musical instrument and play deceivingly with you", i.e. to make Silvius carry her message and at the same time deceive him.

36 *go your way* – "then go".

37 *a tame snake*, i.e. a weak, harmless creature.

38 *charge* – "order".

39 *hence* – "go away".

40 *Good morrow* –"Good morning".

41 *Pray you* – "Please tell me".

42 *purlieus* – "land on the edge".

43 *sheepcote, fenced about with* – "shepherd's cottage surrounded by".

44 *neighbour . . . the place* (line 79) – "next valley; if you pass the row of willow trees *(osiers)* beside the quiet stream, leaving them *(left)* on your right, you will reach the place" *(murmuring* – "making a low sound").

45 *doth keep . . . within* – "is empty; there is no one in it".

190

He that brings this love[31] to thee
Little knows this love in me:
And by him seal[32] up thy mind,
Whether that thy youth and kind
Will the faithful offer take   60
Of me and all that I can make,[33]
Or else by him my love deny,
And then I 'll study[34] how to die."

SILVIUS

Call you this chiding?

CELIA

Alas, poor shepherd!   65

ROSALIND

Do you pity him? No, he deserves no pity. Wilt thou love such
a woman? What, to make thee an instrument,[35] and play false
strains upon thee? Not to be endured! Well, go your way[36] to
her, for I see love hath made thee a tame snake,[37] and say this to
her: that if she love me, I charge[38] her to love thee; if she will   70
not, I will never have her unless thou entreat for her. If you be a
true lover, hence,[39] and not a word; for here comes more
company.   [*Exit* SILVIUS

Enter OLIVER

OLIVER

Good morrow,[40] fair ones. Pray you,[41] if you know,
Where in the purlieus[42] of this forest stands   75
A sheepcote,[43] fenced about with olive trees?

CELIA

West of this place, down in the neighbour bottom;[44]
The rank of osiers by the murmuring stream,
Left on your right hand, brings you to the place.
But at this hour the house doth keep itself,[45]   80
There 's none within.

46 *If that . . . tongue* – "If one may learn to see by what one hears". (Orlando has described Ganymede and Aliena, their clothes and their ages *(years)*; Oliver recognises them from the description.)

47 *Of female favour* – "with a girlish face" (this is Orlando's description of Rosalind).

48 *and bestows . . . sister* – "and he behaves as if he were an older sister". (*ripe* – "grown up", as in "A ripe age", v.i.17).

49 *low, and browner* – "shorter and darker", i.e. smaller and with darker hair, eyes, etc.

50 *no boast, being asked*, i.e. it would have been boastful to say that they were the owners before Oliver asked the question.

51 *doth commend him* – "sends greetings".

52 *napkin* – "handkerchief".

53 *Some of my shame . . . am* – "Something I am ashamed of, if I must tell you what (kind of) man I am".

54 *handkercher* – "handkerchief". Oliver's description of how Orlando saved him makes a lively story with its true-to-life details of the snake's movements and the wild beast's hunger. Its importance to the play lies in the example of human kindness when faced with the cruelty of nature. Compare Duke Senior's generous treatment of Orlando in ii.vii. Such experiences in the Forest of Arden teach the characters of the play the truth about themselves (see Introduction, p. xx).

55 *pacing* – "walking".

56 *Chewing . . . fancy*, i.e. thinking sweet and sad thoughts of love. The image is of a cow slowly using its teeth on *(Chewing)* its food.

57 *Lo, what befell . . . aside* – "Listen to what happened. He looked to one side".

58 *mossed with age* – "covered with moss (smooth green plants growing on trees) because it was old".

59 *bald . . . antiquity* – "without leaves (as a bald head is one without hair) as a result of old age which has dried up the top of the tree".

OLIVER

If that an eye may profit[46] by a tongue,
Then should I know you by description;
Such garments and such years: "The boy is fair,
Of female favour,[47] and bestows[48] himself   85
Like a ripe sister; the woman low,[49]
And browner than her brother." Are not you
The owner of the house I did enquire for?

CELIA

It is no boast, being asked,[50] to say we are.

OLIVER

Orlando doth commend[51] him to you both,   90
And to that youth he calls his Rosalind
He sends this bloody napkin.[52] Are you he?

ROSALIND

I am. What must we understand by this?

OLIVER

Some of my shame,[53] if you will know of me
What man I am, and how and why and where   95
This handkercher[54] was stained.

CELIA

                                   I pray you, tell it.

OLIVER

When last the young Orlando parted from you,
He left a promise to return again
Within an hour; and, pacing[55] through the forest,
Chewing the food[56] of sweet and bitter fancy,   100
Lo, what befell.[57] He threw his eye aside,
And mark what object did present itself.
Under an oak, whose boughs were mossed[58] with age
And high top bald[59] with dry antiquity,

60 *o'ergrown with hair* – "his hair grown too long (through neglect)".

61 *gilded* – "gold-coloured".

62 *wreathed* – "curled".

63 *nimble in threats* – "moving quickly as it threatened harm".

64 *unlinked* – "uncurled".

65 *indented glides* – "in-and-out gliding movements".

66 *drawn dry*, a sign that the lioness was hungry.

67 *couching* – "at full length on the ground".

68 *cat-like . . . When that* – "its eyes were watching, like a cat (watching a bird or mouse), for the time when".

69 *To prey . . . dead :* It was an old belief that the lion (regarded as a "king" of animals) was too noble to touch a creature which seemed to be dead.

70 *This seen* – "when he saw this".

71 *he did render . . . men* – "his description made his brother sound like the most unnatural (in his behaviour as a brother) in the world".

72 *to Orlando* – "let us return to the subject of Orlando".

73 *purposed so* – "had that intention".

74 *kindness* – "natural feeling" (towards a brother). – In the next line, *nature* has the same meaning.

75 *just occasion* – "fair excuse" (for letting Oliver be killed).

76 *fell . . . hurtling* – "was beaten in the fight by Orlando, and during this noisy struggle".

A wretched ragged man, o'ergrown[60] with hair,   105
Lay sleeping on his back; about his neck
A green and gilded[61] snake had wreathed[62] itself,
Who with her head nimble in threats[63] approached
The opening of his mouth; but suddenly,
Seeing Orlando, it unlinked[64] itself,   110
And with indented[65] glides did slip away
Into a bush; under which bush's shade
A lioness, with udders all drawn dry,[66]
Lay couching,[67] head on ground, with catlike[68] watch,
When that the sleeping man should stir; for 't is   115
The royal disposition of that beast
To prey[69] on nothing that doth seem as dead.
This seen,[70] Orlando did approach the man,
And found it was his brother, his elder brother.

CELIA

O, I have heard him speak of that same brother;   120
And he did render[71] him the most unnatural
That lived 'mongst men.

OLIVER

       And well he might so do,
For well I know he was unnatural.

ROSALIND

But, to Orlando:[72] did he leave him there,
Food to the sucked and hungry lioness?   125

OLIVER

Twice did he turn his back and purposed so;[73]
But kindness,[74] nobler ever than revenge,
And nature, stronger than his just occasion,[75]
Made him give battle to the lioness,
Who quickly fell before[76] him; in which hurtling   130
From miserable slumber I awaked.

195

77 *contrive* – "plot".

78 *'t is not I.* i.e. Oliver is not the same person because he has had a change of feelings.

79 *since my . . . thing I am* – "because my change of character *(conversion)*, which has made me the man *(thing)* I am now, is such a sweet experience".

80 *for* – "what about".

81 *By and by* – "(I shall tell you) at once".

82 *When from . . . bathed* – "When in the most natural *(kindly)* way, tears had flowed between *(betwixt)* us during our accounts *(recountments)* of what had happened from first to last".

83 *As how* – "for example, how".

84 *array and entertainment* – "clothing, and food and drink".

85 *Committing me unto* – "placing me in the care of".

86 *here:* Oliver shows on his own arm the place where Orlando had been injured.

87 *cried . . . Rosalind* – "as he was fainting, he called out the name of Rosalind".

88 *recovered him* – "brought him out of his faint".

89 *space* – "amount of time".

90 *in sport* – "jokingly".

196

CELIA

Are you his brother?

ROSALIND

Was 't you he rescued?

CELIA

Was 't you that did so oft contrive[77] to kill him?

OLIVER

'T was I, but 't is not I.[78] I do not shame
To tell you what I was, since my conversion[79]   135
So sweetly tastes, being the thing I am.

ROSALIND

But, for[80] the bloody napkin?

OLIVER

By and by.[81]
When from the first to last,[82] betwixt us two,
Tears our recountments had most kindly bathed –
As how[83] I came into that desert place –   140
In brief, he led me to the gentle Duke,
Who gave me fresh array[84] and entertainment,
Committing[85] me unto my brother's love;
Who led me instantly unto his cave;
There stripped himself; and here,[86] upon his arm   145
The lioness had torn some flesh away,
Which all this while had bled; and now he fainted
And cried, in fainting, upon[87] Rosalind.
Brief, I recovered[88] him, bound up his wound;
And after some small space,[89] being strong at heart,   150
He sent me hither, stranger as I am,
To tell this story, that you might excuse
His broken promise, and to give this napkin,
Dyed in his blood, unto the shepherd youth
That he in sport[90] doth call his Rosalind.   [ROSALIND *faints*   155

197

91 *how now* – "what is the matter".
(Celia pretends to be surprised that
"Ganymede", a man, should faint
at the sight of blood.)

92 *would* – "wish".

93 *Be of good cheer* – "Cheer up".

94 *heart* – "courage".

95 *do so*, i.e. do lack courage.

96 *sirrah . . . this was well counterfeited* –
"sir, anybody would agree that I
pretended very well". Rosalind now
tries to make Oliver believe that her
faint was pretended, so that he will
continue to think that she is a man.
(*Counterfeit*, here and in lines 165,
166, 168 and 169 – "(make a) pretence".)

97 *Heigh-ho*, an expression of amusement.

98 *there is too . . . earnest* – "the colour of
your face (i.e. its paleness) bears witness *(testimony)* too plainly that it
was real suffering *(a passion of
earnest)*".

99 *a good heart* – "courage".

CELIA

Why, how now,[91] Ganymede, sweet Ganymede!

OLIVER

Many will swoon when they do look on blood.

CELIA

There is more in it. Cousin! Ganymede!

OLIVER

Look, he recovers.

ROSALIND

I would[92] I were at home.

CELIA

We'll lead you thither.   160
I pray you, will you take him by the arm?

OLIVER

Be of good cheer,[93] youth. You a man! You lack a man's heart.[94]

ROSALIND

I do so,[95] I conféss it. Ah, sirrah,[96] a body would think this was
well counterfeited. I pray you tell your brother how well I
counterfeited. [*She laughs*] Heigh-ho![97]   165

OLIVER

This was not counterfeit; there is too great testimony[98] in your
complexion that it was a passion of earnest.

ROSALIND

Counterfeit, I assure you.

OLIVER

Well then, take a good heart[99] and counterfeit to be a man.

100 *draw* – "come".
101 *How you excuse* – "whether you forgive" (for missing his appointment).
102 *Rosalind* – Oliver uses Rosalind's real name, showing that he now understands she is not the boy "Ganymede".

103 *commend my counterfeiting* – "praise my skill in pretending (to faint)".

ROSALIND

So I do; but, i' faith, I should have been a woman by right. 170

CELIA

Come, you look paler and paler; pray you draw[100] homewards.
Good sir, go with us.

OLIVER

That will I, for I must bear answer back
How you excuse[101] my brother, Rosalind.[102]

ROSALIND

I shall devise something; but I pray you commend[103] my 175
counterfeiting to him. Will you go?

[*Exeunt*

(v.i) Touchstone and Audrey meet William, Audrey's former lover. Touchstone pretends to be a very learned man; he threatens William and orders him to give up Audrey. William cheerfully agrees to do so.

1 *a time*, i.e. for marriage.
2 *for all . . . saying* – "in spite of what was said by the old gentleman" (i.e. Jaques – III.iii.66–70).
3 *interest in* – "claim to".
4 *meat and drink* – "great satisfaction".
5 *clown*, i.e. a simple country fellow.
6 *By my troth* – "Indeed".
7 *we that have . . . hold* (line 10) – "those of us who have clever minds are greatly to blame: we insist on mocking others *(flouting)*; we cannot restrain ourselves".

8 *even* – "evening" (also in lines 11–14).
9 *God ye good even* – "God give you a good evening".

ACT V

Scene I. The forest.

Enter TOUCHSTONE *and* AUDREY.

TOUCHSTONE

We shall find a time,[1] Audrey; patience, gentle Audrey.

AUDREY

Faith, the priest was good enough, for all the old gentleman's[2] saying.

TOUCHSTONE

A most wicked Sir Oliver, Audrey, a most vile Mar-text. But, Audrey, there is a youth here in the forest lays claim to you.   5

AUDREY

Ay, I know who 't is: he hath no interest[3] in me in the world. Here comes the man you mean.

Enter WILLIAM

TOUCHSTONE

It is meat and drink[4] to me to see a clown.[5] By my troth,[6] we that have good wits[7] have much to answer for; we shall be flouting; we cannot hold.   10

WILLIAM

Good even,[8] Audrey.

AUDREY

God ye[9] good even, William.

WILLIAM

And good even to you, sir.

10 *Cover thy head* – "Put your cap on (again)". (Touchstone is playing the great courtier being gracious to the simple peasant. He has already tried this on Jaques – III.iii.60-1.)

11 *so so* – "fairly (rich)".

12 *but so so* – "only fairly good (as an answer)".

13 *pretty wit* – "good intelligence".

14 *The heathen philosopher:* Touchstone is not referring to any actual person, but talks in this way to make William respect him as a learned man; the "philosophy" is just common sense.

15 *thereby* – "by doing so".

TOUCHSTONE

Good even, gentle friend. Cover[10] thy head, cover thy head;
nay, prithee, be covered. How old are you, friend?   15

WILLIAM

Five and twenty, sir.

TOUCHSTONE

A ripe age. Is thy name William?

WILLIAM

William, sir.

TOUCHSTONE

A fair name. Wast born i' the forest here?

WILLIAM

Ay, sir, I thank God.   20

TOUCHSTONE

"Thank God"; a good answer. Art rich?

WILLIAM

Faith, sir, so so.[11]

TOUCHSTONE

"So so" is good, very good, very excellent good; and yet it is
not; it is but so so.[12] Art thou wise?

WILLIAM

Ay, sir, I have a pretty[13] wit.   25

TOUCHSTONE

Why, thou sayest well. I do now remember a saying, "The fool
doth think he is wise, but the wise man knows himself to be a
fool." The heathen[14] philosopher, when he had a desire to eat a
grape, would open his lips when he put it into his mouth;
meaning thereby[15] that grapes were made to eat and lips to open.   30
You do love this maid?

16 *a figure in rhetoric* – "a recognised and respected argument". *Rhetoric* was the study of good style in writing or public speaking; a *figure* was one of the recognised "figures of speech" (e.g. metaphor, simile) which give force to what is said. Touchstone's "figure" here has no purpose; it tells what everyone knows.

17 *your writers* – "well-known writers".

18 *ipse*, Latin for "he (himself)".

19 *the vulgar* – "the speech of uneducated people". (Touchstone "translates" his fine words for William. Both *the boorish*, in line 42, and *the common*, in line 43, have the same meaning as *the vulgar*.)

20 *to thy better understanding*, "so that you will better understand my meaning".

21 *to wit* – "in other words".

22 *make thee away* – "destroy you"; "kill you".

23 *translate* – "change".

24 *bandy . . . faction* – "argue with you like a politician". (This would not ordinarily cause death, but since William does not know what it means, it will have its effect in frightening him. The same is true of *o'er-run thee with policy* – "defeat you by cunning".)

25 *rest you merry* – "keep you happy" (i.e. "good-bye").

I do, sir.

TOUCHSTONE

Give me your hand. Art thou learned?

WILLIAM

No, sir.

TOUCHSTONE

Then learn this of me: to have is to have; for it is a figure[16] in   35
rhetoric that drink, being poured out of a cup into a glass, by
filling the one doth empty the other; for all your writers[17]
do consent that *ipse*[18] is he. Now, you are not *ipse*, for I am he.

WILLIAM

Which he, sir?

TOUCHSTONE

He, sir, that must marry this woman. Therefore, you clown,   40
abandon – which is in the vulgar,[19] leave – the society – which
in the boorish is, company – of this female – which in the
common is, woman. Which together is, abandon the society
of this female, or, clown, thou perishest; or, to thy better understanding,[20] diest; or, to wit,[21] I kill thee, make thee away,[22]   45
translate[23] thy life into death, thy liberty into bondage. I will
deal in poison with thee, or in bastinado, or in steel; I will bandy
with thee in faction;[24] I will o'er-run thee with policy; I will
kill thee a hundred and fifty ways: therefore tremble and
depart.   50

AUDREY

Do, good William.

WILLIAM

God rest you merry,[25] sir.   [*Exit*

26 *Trip* – "Run".   27 *attend* – "am going with you".

(v.ii) Oliver tells Orlando that he and "Aliena" (Celia) have fallen in love with each other at first sight. He wants to give up to Orlando their father's house and wealth, and to live with Aliena like a shepherd in the forest. Rosalind, still in disguise, meets Orlando and promises that the real Rosalind will come and marry him tomorrow. She also promises Phebe that if "Ganymede" ever marries any woman, it will be Phebe.

1 *on . . . acquaintance*, i.e. after knowing her for so short a time.

2 *wooing . . . grant* – "when you wooed her, she agreed (to marry you)".

3 *persever to enjoy her* – "continue (*persever*, pronounced per-sév-er) with the affair in order to marry her".

4 *Neither . . . question* – "Do not raise objections to *(call in question)* the suddenness *(giddiness)* of it".

5 *small* – "short".

6 *say with me* – "agree with me when I say" (similarly, line 7, *say with her* – "agree with her . . .").

7 *enjoy* – "marry and live happily with".

8 *revenue* (pronounced re-vén-ue) – "money from rents etc."

9 *estate upon* – "give by law to".

10 *all 's* – "all his".

11 *God . . . brother*, a greeting. Rosalind, as Ganymede, calls the future husband of her "sister", Aliena, *brother*. In reply, Oliver again shows he knows "Ganymede" is a girl by greeting "him" – as *sister*.

Enter CORIN

CORIN

Our master and mistress seeks you: come away, away!

TOUCHSTONE

Trip,[26] Audrey! Trip, Audrey! I attend,[27] I attend.   [*Exeunt*

Scene II. The forest.

Enter ORLANDO *and* OLIVER.

ORLANDO

Is 't possible that on so little acquaintance[1] you should like her? That but seeing, you should love her? And loving, woo? And wooing, she should grant?[2] And will you persever[3] to enjoy her?

OLIVER

Neither call the giddiness[4] of it in question, the poverty of   5
her, the small[5] acquaintance, my sudden wooing, nor her sudden consenting; but say with me,[6] I love Aliena; say with her, that she loves me; consent with both, that we may enjoy[7] each other. It shall be to your good; for my father's house, and all the revenue[8] that was old Sir Rowland's, will I estate[9] upon you,   10
and here live and die a shepherd.

Enter ROSALIND

ORLANDO

You have my consent. Let your wedding be tomorrow: thither will I invite the Duke and all 's[10] contented followers. Go you and prepare Aliena; for look you, here comes my Rosalind.

ROSALIND

God save you, brother.[11]   15

209

12 *wear thy heart in a scarf*: Orlando has a scarf (a long strip of cloth) round his wounded arm, but Rosalind speaks of him jokingly as a lover "wounded" in the heart, and wearing a scarf over it as a bandage.

13 *counterfeited . . . handkercher*: See iv.iii.163ff. and notes.

14 *where are you* – "what you mean" (i.e. that Oliver and Celia have fallen in love).

15 *fight of two rams*: Two *rams* (male sheep) seem to attack each other suddenly and without cause. It is the suddenness that Rosalind wants her image to suggest.

16 *Caesar's . . . overcame*: Julius Caesar sent the very short message, *Veni, vidi, vici*, meaning *I came, saw, and overcame* (conquered), to inform Rome of his victory in 47 B.C. It is described by Rosalind as a great boast (*thrasonical*, from the name of Thraso, a famous boaster in a Roman play by Terence; *brag* – "boast") and another example of suddenness (the three words were a very "sudden" way of reporting a campaign).

17 *no sooner met, but* – "as soon as they met" (and similarly in the following lines).

18 *in these degrees* – "in this way, step by step".

19 *a pair of stairs* – "staircase"; "set of stairs" (with word-play on moving step by step).

20 *incontinent* – "immediately". (The word has a second meaning, "without control", which is the sense in which it is used in the last part of the sentence.)

21 *wrath* – "fury" (like the two rams, line 26, which cannot be kept apart even if they are beaten with thick sticks, *clubs* – line 35).

22 *will together* – "must be together".

OLIVER

And you, fair sister.   [*Exit*

ROSALIND

O my dear Orlando, how it grieves me to see thee wear thy
heart in a scarf![12]

ORLANDO

It is my arm.

ROSALIND

I thought thy heart had been wounded with the claws of a lion.   20

ORLANDO

Wounded it is, but with the eyes of a lady.

ROSALIND

Did your brother tell you how I counterfeited[13] to swoon when
he showed me your handkercher?

ORLANDO

Ay, and greater wonders than that.

ROSALIND

O, I know where you are![14] Nay, 't is true: there was never   25
anything so sudden but the fight of two rams,[15] and Caesar's
thrasonical[16] brag of "I came, saw, and overcame"; for your
brother and my sister no sooner[17] met, but they looked; no
sooner looked, but they loved; no sooner loved, but they sighed;
no sooner sighed, but they asked one another the reason; no   30
sooner knew the reason, but they sought the remedy; and in
these degrees[18] have they made a pair of stairs[19] to marriage,
which they will climb incontinent,[20] or else be incontinent
before marriage. They are in the very wrath[21] of love, and they
will together;[22] clubs cannot part them.   35

211

23 *bid . . . nuptial* – "invite the Duke to the wedding".

24 *to look . . . man's eyes,* i.e. to know what happiness is by watching another man's (while remaining unhappy oneself).

25 *By so much . . . wishes for* (line 40) – "The more I think tomorrow about my brother's being happy because he has what he wants, the more extreme will my own sadness *(heartheaviness)* become".

26 *serve your . . . Rosalind* – "take the place of (the real) Rosalind for you".

27 *by thinking,* i.e. by imagination, not reality.

28 *idle* – "useless".

29 *to some purpose* – "in a practical way".

30 *conceit* – "intelligence"; "understanding". Rosalind then explains (lines 45–49): "I have not said that I know you are (a man of intelligence) just to gain your good opinion of *my* intelligence *(knowledge)*; nor am I trying to gain *(labour for)* your respect, except in the amount necessary to make you believe me – for your own good, not so that you will honour me".

31 *conversed* – "spent my time".

32 *not damnable* – "not deserving eternal punishment" (for practising magic, because it is good magic not used for harmful purposes).

33 *so near . . . cries it out* – "as sincerely as your behaviour *(gesture)* plainly indicates".

34 *straits of fortune* – "misfortunes and difficulties" (the image is of a ship driven by the storm into a narrow passage between dangerous rocks).

35 *if it appear . . . to you* – i.e. "if you really want me to do it".

36 *human . . . danger* – "as a real person, and without any risk (such as one might fear as the result of using magic)".

37 *Speakest . . . meanings* – "Do you seriously mean what you say".

38 *tender . . . magician* – "value greatly, even if I am a magician". (Magicians, like witches, were sometimes punished with death.)

39 *array* – "clothes".

40 *bid* – "invite".

ORLANDO

They shall be married tomorrow, and I will bid[23] the Duke to the nuptial. But, O, how bitter a thing it is to look into happiness[24] through another man's eyes! By so much the more[25] shall I tomorrow be at the height of heart-heaviness, by how much I shall think my brother happy in having what he wishes for.   40

ROSALIND

Why then, tomorrow I cannot serve your turn[26] for Rosalind?

ORLANDO

I can live no longer by thinking.[27]

ROSALIND

I will weary you then no longer with idle[28] talking. Know of me then, for now I speak to some purpose,[29] that I know you are a gentleman of good conceit.[30] I speak not this that you should   45 bear a good opinion of my knowledge, insomuch I say I know you are; neither do I labour for a greater esteem than may in some little measure draw a belief from you, to do yourself good, and not to grace me. Believe then, if you please, that I can do strange things. I have, since I was three years old, conversed[31]   50 with a magician, most profound in his art and yet not damnable.[32] If you do love Rosalind so near the heart as your gesture[33] cries it out, when your brother marries Aliena, shall you marry her. I know into what straits[34] of fortune she is driven; and it is not impossible to me, if it appear not inconvenient[35] to you, to   55 set her before your eyes tomorrow, human[36] as she is, and without any danger.

ORLANDO

Speakest thou in sober[37] meanings?

ROSALIND

By my life, I do; which I tender[38] dearly, though I say I am a magician. Therefore put you in your best array;[39] bid[40] your   60

213

41 *will* – "want to".

42 *done . . . ungentleness* – "treated me in a way not at all suitable for a gentleman".

43 *writ* – "wrote".

44 *study* – "serious intention".

45 *despiteful* – "scornful".

friends; for if you will[41] be married tomorrow, you shall; and to Rosalind, if you will.

Enter SILVIUS *and* PHEBE

Look, here comes a lover of mine and a lover of hers.

PHEBE

Youth, you have done me much ungentleness,[42]
To show the letter that I writ[43] to you.   65

ROSALIND

I care not if I have: it is my study[44]
To seem despiteful[45] and ungentle to you.
You are there followed by a faithful shepherd;
Look upon him, love him; he worships you.

PHEBE

Good shepherd, tell this youth what 't is to love.   70

SILVIUS

It is to be all made of sighs and tears;
And so am I for Phebe.

PHEBE

And I for Ganymede.

ORLANDO

And I for Rosalind.

ROSALIND

And I for no woman.   75

SILVIUS

It is to be all made of faith and service;
And so am I for Phebe.

215

46 *fantasy* - "thoughts of love".

47 *observance* - "respectful service". (The word *observance* appears in line 85, and some editors see it as a printer's mistake there and substitute *obedience*.)

48 *patience, and impatience*, i.e. patience in bearing unkindness, but impatience in wishing for an acceptance of one's love.

49 *blame . . . love you* - "do you blame me for loving you".

50 *Who do you speak to:* Orlando does not know that Rosalind herself is present.

The first edition has *Why . . . too*, which is not the question that Orlando answers, and was probably a printer's mistake due to the frequency of "Why" in this conversation.

PHEBE

And I for Ganymede.

ORLANDO

And I for Rosalind.

ROSALIND

And I for no woman.   80

SILVIUS

It is to be all made of fantasy,[46]
All made of passion, and all made of wishes;
All adoration, duty, and observance,[47]
All humbleness, all patience, and impatience,[48]
All purity, all trial, all observance;   85
And so am I for Phebe.

PHEBE

And so am I for Ganymede.

ORLANDO

And so am I for Rosalind.

ROSALIND

And so am I for no woman.

PHEBE

[*To* ROSALIND] If this be so, why blame you me[49] to love you?   90

SILVIUS

[*To* PHEBE] If this be so, why blame you me to love you?

ORLANDO

[*Aside*] If this be so, why blame you me to love you?

ROSALIND

Who do you speak to,[50] "Why blame you me to love you?"

217

51 *the howling . . . moon:* There was a belief that wolves howled more on moonlight nights than at other times. Rosalind compares the unchanging repetition of the same words by Silvius, Phebe, and Orlando, to the unchanging sound of wolves howling at night. There were stretches of very wild country in Ireland; this seems to be the reason for the mention of *Irish*.

52 *satisfy* – "keep my promise to".
53 *I have . . . commands* – "I have given you your orders".

(v.iii) Two pages (boy attendants) sing to Touchstone and Audrey the song "It was a lover and his lass".

1 *dishonest* – "shameful".
2 *woman of the world* – "married woman" (belonging to the life of the world: having children and making homes. See v.iv.35 and note 11).

ORLANDO

To her that is not here, nor doth not hear.

ROSALIND

Pray you, no more of this; 't is like the howling of Irish wolves[51]   95
against the moon. *To* SILVIUS] I will help you if I can.
[*To* PHEBE] I would love you if I could. – Tomorrow meet me
all together. [*To* PHEBE] I will marry you, if ever I marry
woman, and I 'll be married tomorrow. [*To* ORLANDO] I will
satisfy[52] you, if ever I satisfied man, and you shall be married 100
tomorrow. [*To* SILVIUS] I will content you, if what pleases
you contents you, and you shall be married tomorrow. [*To*
ORLANDO] As you love Rosalind, meet. [*To* SILVIUS] As
you love Phebe, meet. And as I love no woman, I 'll meet. So
fare you well; I have left you commands.[53]   105

SILVIUS

I 'll not fail, if I live.

PHEBE

Nor I.

ORLANDO

Nor I.   [*Exeunt*

Scene III. *The forest.*

Enter TOUCHSTONE *and* AUDREY.

TOUCHSTONE

Tomorrow is the joyful day, Audrey; tomorrow will we be
married.

AUDREY

I do desire it with all my heart; and I hope it is no dishonest[1]
desire to desire to be a woman of the world.[2] Here come two of
the banished Duke's pages.   5

3 *Well met* – "I am glad to meet you" (a common greeting).

4 *By my troth* – "Indeed".

5 *for* – "in agreement with" (i.e. glad to sing for).

6 *clap . . . roundly* – "start it (the song) directly".

7 *the only . . . voice* – "always the excuses made in advance for having a bad singing voice" (*prologues*, literally, speeches made before the play begins).

8 *I' faith* – "Indeed".

9 *in a tune . . . horse*, i.e. both singing together and keeping good time, like two *gipsies* (see Glossary) on the same horse: the one horse that both ride being like the one tune that both sing.

10 *With a hey . . . nonino:* The words have no meaning; like *hey ding . . . ding* in the fifth line, they are only sounds to be sung to the tune of the song.

11 *ring time* – "time for giving wedding rings" (or for exchanging rings as love tokens).

12 *Between . . . rye*, i.e. in the unsown ground (usually covered with grass and wild flowers) running between, and separating, the strips sown with rye (the kind of corn usually grown for bread in Shakespeare's time).

13 *&c.*, i.e. the rest of the first verse is repeated.

14 *carol* – "song".

15 *that hour* – "at that time".

like two gipsies on a horse

Enter two Pages

FIRST PAGE

[*To* TOUCHSTONE] Well met,[3] honest gentleman.

TOUCHSTONE

By my troth,[4] well met. Come, sit, sit and a song.

SECOND PAGE

We are for[5] you; sit i' th' middle.

FIRST PAGE

Shall we clap[6] into 't roundly, without hawking or spitting or saying we are hoarse, which are the only[7] prologues to a bad 10 voice?

SECOND PAGE

I' faith,[8] i' faith; and both in a tune,[9] like two gipsies on a horse.

Song

It was a lover and his lass,
　　With a hey,[10] and a ho, and a hey nonino,　　　　15
That o'er the green cornfield did pass
　　In the spring time, the only pretty ring time,[11]
When birds do sing, hey ding a ding, ding;
　　Sweet lovers love the spring.

Between the acres[12] of the rye,　　　　20
　　With a hey, and a ho, and a hey nonino,
These pretty country folks would lie,
　　In the spring time, &c.[13]

This carol[14] they began that hour,[15]
　　With a hey, and a ho, and a hey nonino,　　　　25
How that a life was but a flower
　　In the spring time, &c.

16 *take* – "seize and use".

17 *love . . . prime* – "love is at its best *(crowned)* in the spring *(prime)*".

18 *no great . . . untuneable* – "not much meaning *(matter)* in the words of the song *(ditty)*, it was sung very much out of tune".

19 *deceived* – "mistaken".

20 *we kept time*, with two meanings: (i) "We kept time in our singing" (sang together); (ii) "kept singing about *time*" (i.e. *spring time, ring time, the present time*).

21 *time lost* – "waste of time".

22 *God buy . . . voices* – "Good-bye, and may God improve your singing".

(v.iv) All are waiting for Rosalind to arrive and fulfil her promises. Meanwhile, Touchstone entertains Jaques with mockery of the fashion for quarrels and duels. Celia and Rosalind arrive, together with the god Hymen, who has come from heaven. Rosalind, no longer in disguise, makes herself known to her father and Orlando. Phebe realises that "Ganymede", as a girl, will marry no woman, and accepts the faithful Silvius instead. Hymen marries all the four pairs of lovers. In the end, Jaques de Boys, Orlando's other brother, arrives and tells Duke Senior that his brother Frederick has been persuaded to give up his rule and devote himself to religion. Duke Senior and all his friends, except Jaques, prepare to return to court; Jaques decides instead to join Frederick in his new way of life.

1 *the boy*, i.e. "Ganymede".

2 *As those . . . hope* – "like those people who are afraid that their hopes will come to nothing".

3 *whiles our . . . urged* – "while our agreement *(compact)* is stated again". (Rosalind is still disguised as "Ganymede". The agreement was reached partly in v.ii.98–105, but Rosalind has spoken since then to Duke Senior, to Phebe again, and to Silvius.)

4 *bestow her on* – "give her as wife to".

222

And therefore take[16] the present time,
   With a hey, and a ho, and a hey nonino,
For love is crownéd[17] with the prime,   30
   In the spring time, &c.

TOUCHSTONE

Truly, young gentlemen, though there was no great matter[18] in
the ditty, yet the note was very untuneable.

FIRST PAGE

You are deceived,[19] sir: we kept time;[20] we lost not our time.

TOUCHSTONE

By my troth, yes; I count it but time lost[21] to hear such a   35
foolish song. God buy you, and God mend[22] your voices. Come,
Audrey.   [*Exeunt*

Scene IV. The forest.

Enter DUKE SENIOR, AMIENS, JAQUES, ORLANDO,
OLIVER *and* CELIA.

DUKE SENIOR

Dost thou believe, Orlando, that the boy[1]
Can do all this that he hath promiséd?

ORLANDO

I sometimes do believe, and sometimes do not;
As those that fear they hope,[2] and know they fear.

Enter ROSALIND, SILVIUS *and* PHEBE

ROSALIND

Patience once more, whiles our compact[3] is urged.   5
[*To* DUKE SENIOR] You say, if I bring in your Rosalind,
You will bestow[4] her on Orlando here?

5 *Though . . . one thing* – "Even if I had
  to die to have her".
6 *make all . . . even* – "settle this whole
  affair" (*make even*, meaning "settle",
  appears again in line 25).

DUKE SENIOR

That would I, had I kingdoms to give with her.

ROSALIND

[*To* ORLANDO] And you say, you will have her when I bring her?

ORLANDO

That would I, were I of all kingdoms king.   10

ROSALIND

[*To* PHEBE] You say you 'll marry me, if I be willing?

PHEBE

That will I, should I die the hour after.

ROSALIND

But if you do refuse to marry me,
You 'll give yourself to this most faithful shepherd?

PHEBE

So is the bargain.   15

ROSALIND

[*To* SILVIUS] You say that you 'll have Phebe, if she will?

SILVIUS

Though to have her and death[5] were both one thing.

ROSALIND

I have promised to make all this matter even.[6]
Keep you your word, O Duke, to give your daughter:
You yours, Orlando, to receive his daughter: 20
Keep you your word, Phebe, that you 'll marry me,
Or else, refusing me, to wed this shepherd:
Keep your word, Silvius, that you 'll marry her
If she refuse me: and from hence I go,
To make these doubts all even.   [*Exeunt* ROSALIND *and* CELIA   25

7 *I do remember . . . favour* – "This shepherd boy's face reminds me strongly of my daughter's face *(favour)* in some ways".

8 *Methought he was* – "He seemed to me just like".

9 *tutored . . . studies* – "taught the essential ideas *(rudiments)* of many dangerous subjects of study".

10 *Obscured in the circle* – "hidden in the area". (There is also a suggestion of the circles drawn by magicians, inside which they made themselves invisible.)

11 *another flood toward* – "another great flood going to happen". The reference is to the account in the Bible of the great flood (pouring down of water) which covered the earth (*Genesis* 6–8), when one pair *(couple)* of each of the kinds of animals entered the ship *(ark)* built by Noah, so that life could continue when the flood ended. The idea is that marriage, through which children are born, is like an ark that saves humanity from being destroyed by the "flood" of time.

12 *tongues* – "languages".

13 *Salutation* – "A solemn greeting".

14 *motley-minded*, i.e. with a mind full of ideas (which, Jaques suggests, are as mixed as the colours of his clothes).

15 *put . . . purgation* – "test me thoroughly".

16 *measure*, i.e. a slow, court dance.

17 *politic* – "cunning".

18 *smooth* – "polite". (One would expect a man to be cunning *(politic)* in dealing with his enemy, and polite to his friend. Touchstone suggests that a courtier has to reverse this order.)

19 *undone* – "ruined" (by not paying their bills).

20 *like to . . . one* – "nearly came to fighting because of one of them", i.e. there was almost a duel (a fight between two persons, usually with swords, to settle a quarrel).

21 *ta'en up* – "settled (without a fight)".

I have had four quarrels, and like to[20] *have fought one*

DUKE SENIOR

I do remember in this shepherd boy
Some lively[7] touches of my daughter's favour

ORLANDO

My lord, the first time that I ever saw him,
Methought[8] he was a brother to your daughter.
But, my good lord, this boy is forest-born,   30
And hath been tutored[9] in the rudiments
Of many desperate studies by his uncle,
Whom he reports to be a great magician,
Obscuréd[10] in the circle of this forest.

Enter TOUCHSTONE *and* AUDREY

JAQUES

There is, sure, another flood toward,[11] and these couples are   35
coming to the ark. Here comes a pair of very strange beasts,
which in all tongues[12] are called fools.

TOUCHSTONE

Salutation[13] and greeting to you all!

JAQUES

Good my lord, bid him welcome. This is the motley-minded[14]
gentleman that I have so often met in the forest. He hath been   40
a courtier, he swears.

TOUCHSTONE

If any man doubt that, let him put me to my purgation.[15] I
have trod a measure;[16] I have flattered a lady; I have been
politic[17] with my friend, smooth[18] with mine enemy; I have
undone[19] three tailors; I have had four quarrels, and like to[20]   45
have fought one.

JAQUES

And how was that ta'en up?[21]

227

22 *How* – "What do you mean by".

23 *'ield*, for *yield* – "reward" (said to Duke Senior).

24 *I desire . . . like* – "I wish you the same" (said to Jaques in thanks for speaking well of him).

25 *I press . . . blood breaks* – "I have joined the crowd of other pairs of country people who are to be married *(copulatives)*, in order to swear to be faithful to one person and (then) give up my promise *(forswear)* according to the way marriage binds us together and my desires *(blood)* cause me to break my promise". This is a joke of Touchstone's to the audience, not a serious statement to the Duke.

26 *ill-favoured thing* – "unbeautiful object (i.e. person)".

27 *a poor humour* – "a humble fancy".

28 *that that . . . will* – "what no other man wants".

29 *Rich honesty* – "Great virtue". (A woman's unattractive appearance may hide a virtuous mind, Touchstone says, just as a poor-looking house may hide the wealth of a miser – who hates spending money – or as the unattractive shell of an oyster may hide a valuable pearl.)

30 *swift and sententious* – "quick with sayings that are full of meaning".

31 *the fool's bolt*: This refers to the saying, "A fool's bolt (arrow) is soon shot", i.e. a fool speaks quickly about what is in his mind. Touchstone is humble about his quick answers, describing them as one of the pleasant weaknesses *(dulcet diseases)* that fools have.

32 *for*, i.e. to return to the subject of.

33 *Upon . . . removed*, i.e. by seven ways of accusing a man of lying without directly calling him a liar. Touchstone describes how he and a courtier insulted each other six times, progressing nearer to but not reaching the seventh time, when one would call the other a liar, and so cause a duel. By listing the different kinds of insult like rules in grammar, Touchstone makes the fashion of duelling look foolish and nonsensical.

34 *bear . . . seeming* – "stand more gracefully".

35 *as thus* – "in this way".

36 *did dislike the cut* – "expressed my dislike of the shape (which was the result of cutting)".

37 *in the mind* – "of the opinion that".

38 *Retort Courteous*, i.e. polite reply.

39 *Quip Modest*, i.e. moderate answer.

40 *If again* – "If I said again".

your pearl in your foul oyster

TOUCHSTONE

Faith, we met, and found the quarrel was upon the seventh cause.

JAQUES

How[22] seventh cause? Good my lord, like this fellow.

DUKE SENIOR

I like him very well.   50

TOUCHSTONE

God 'ield[23] you, sir; I desire you of the like.[24] I press[25] in here,
sir, amongst the rest of the country copulatives, to swear and
to forswear, according as marriage binds and blood breaks.
A poor virgin, sir, an ill-favoured[26] thing, sir, but mine own;
a poor humour[27] of mine, sir, to take that that[28] no man else   55
will. Rich honesty[29] dwells like a miser, sir, in a poor house, as
your pearl in your foul oyster.

DUKE SENIOR

By my faith, he is very swift[30] and sententious.

TOUCHSTONE

According to the fool's bolt,[31] sir, and such dulcet diseases.

JAQUES

But, for[32] the seventh cause; how did you find the quarrel on   60
the seventh cause?

TOUCHSTONE

Upon a lie[33] seven times removed – bear your body more
seeming,[34] Audrey – as thus,[35] sir. I did dislike the cut[36] of a
certain courtier's beard: he sent me word, if I said his beard was
not cut well, he was in the mind[37] it was: this is called the   65
Retort Courteous.[38] If I sent him word again, "it was not well
cut", he would send me word, he cut it to please himself: this
is called the Quip Modest.[39] If again,[40] "it was not well cut",

41 *disabled* – "said that he did not value".

42 *Reply Churlish*, i.e. rude reply.

43 *spake not true* – "was not speaking the truth".

44 *Reproof Valiant*, i.e. fearless blaming.

45 *Countercheck Quarrelsome*, i.e. denial leading to a quarrel.

46 *Lie Circumstantial*, i.e. indirect way of saying a person is lying.

47 *durst* – "dared".

48 *nor he . . . give me* – "and he did not dare to answer me with".

49 *measured swords:* The length of swords was measured before a duel to make sure that they were equal. To part without fighting after measuring swords was most improbable.

50 *nominate . . . the lie* – "name the different ways of telling someone he lies in order of seriousness".

51 *in print, by the book* – "in a very exact way (in print), according to the rules in the book". A number of books on the art of quarrelling and duelling were printed towards the end of the sixteenth century. There were other books which taught the rules of (*books for* – line 80) *good manners*. Touchstone's point is that books teaching the art of quarrelling taught *bad* manners.

52 *avoid but* – "avoid fighting about, except".

53 *justices . . . swore brothers* (line 90) – "judges could not find a way of settling (*take up*) a quarrel, but when the two persons concerned (*parties*) met (in order to fight the duel), one of them happened to think (*thought but*) of the word *If* to add – *If* you said something, then I answered with something else – and they shook hands and swore to behave like brothers". (When *If* was added, there was no direct statement; the whole quarrel could then appear to have been caused by a misunderstanding.)

54 *rare* – "splendid".

he disabled[41] my judgment: this is called the Reply Churlish.[42]
If again, "it was not well cut", he would answer, I spake[43]   70
not true: this is called the Reproof Valiant.[44] If again, "it
was not well cut", he would say I lie: this is called the Countercheck Quarrelsome:[45] and so to the Lie Circumstantial[46] and
the Lie Direct.

JAQUES

And how oft did you say his beard was not well cut?   75

TOUCHSTONE

I durst[47] go no further than the Lie Circumstantial, nor[48] he
durst not give me the Lie Direct; and so we measured swords[49]
and parted.

JAQUES

Can you nominate[50] in order now the degrees of the lie?

TOUCHSTONE

O sir, we quarrel in print,[51] by the book, as you have books   80
for good manners: I will name you the degrees. The first, the
Retort Courteous; the second, the Quip Modest; the third, the
Reply Churlish; the fourth, the Reproof Valiant; the fifth,
the Countercheck Quarrelsome; the sixth, the Lie with Cir-
cumstance; the seventh, the Lie Direct. All these you may   85
avoid[52] but the Lie Direct, and you may avoid that, too, with
an "If". I knew when seven justices[53] could not take up a quarrel,
but when the parties were met themselves, one of them thought
but of an "If": as, "If you said so, then I said so"; and they
shook hands and swore brothers. Your "If" is the only peace-   90
maker; much virtue in If.

JAQUES

Is not this a rare[54] fellow, my lord? He 's as good at anything,
and yet a fool.

55 *He uses . . . shoots his wit*: The image is of a man hunting duck and other wild birds and using an old horse, or the figure of one made from cloth, to hide behind; the birds would not be afraid of this *stalking-horse*, and so the hunter could get close to them to shoot them. Duke Senior says that Touchstone hides behind his appearance *(presentation)* of foolishness, so that he may have a chance to attack people more effectively with his real cleverness.

56 *HYMEN*, the Roman god of marriage (who has come down from heaven). Shakespeare's audiences did not, of course, believe in the existence of the ancient gods, but they were used to the personification of ideas by actors on the stage. Hymen's presence as a god helped to express the idea of marriage as a holy condition and heaven's way of bringing harmony to human beings on earth. See Introduction, p. xxiii.

57 *is there mirth* – "there is rejoicing".

58 *When earthly . . . together* – "when with problems on earth solved *(made even)*, all things are made to agree *(Atone* – literally, 'make at one')".

59 *Hymen . . . brought her* – "Hymen, (who has) come down from heaven, has brought her".

60 *That thou . . . bosom is* – "so that you can give her in marriage to the man whose heart is already hers" (literally, put her hand into the hand of the man whose heart is already in her heart).

61 *To you . . . yours* (line 105): Rosalind declares that she owes service and loyalty (i) to Duke Senior, her father and (ii) to Orlando, her husband.

62 *If there . . . sight* – "If what I see is true" (also in line 107).

63 *my love adieu* – "goodbye to my love", i.e. that is the end of my love (since "Ganymede" is the girl Rosalind).

64 *if you be not she* – "unless that woman is yourself". Rosalind keeps her promise (v.ii.98-9), though not in the way expected.

*like a stalking horse*55

232

DUKE SENIOR

He uses his folly like a stalking-horse,[55] and under the presentation of that he shoots his wit.   95

Enter HYMEN,[56] ROSALIND *and* CELIA (*neither now
in disguise*). *Soft music*

HYMEN

> Then is there mirth[57] in heaven,
> When earthly things made even[58]
>   Atone together.
> Good Duke, receive thy daughter;
> Hymen from heaven[59] brought her,   100
>   Yea, brought her hither,
> That thou mightst join her hand with his[60]
> Whose heart within her bosom is.

ROSALIND

[*To* DUKE] To you[61] I give myself, for I am yours.
[*To* ORLANDO] To you I give myself, for I am yours.   105

DUKE SENIOR

If there be truth in sight,[62] you are my daughter.

ORLANDO

If there be truth in sight, you are my Rosalind.

PHEBE

If sight and shape be true,
Why then, my love adieu![63]

ROSALIND

[*To* DUKE] I 'll have no father, if you be not he.   110
[*To* ORLANDO] I 'll have no husband, if you be not he.
[*To* PHEBE] Nor ne'er wed woman, if you be not she.[64]

65 *Peace ho! I bar* – "Silence. I forbid".

66 *Hymen's bands*, i.e. the bond of marriage.

67 *If truth . . . contents* – "if the truth really is true".

68 *no cross shall part* – "shall never be separated by any quarrel *(cross)*".

69 *heart in heart* – "completely united in love".

70 *You to . . . lord* – "You (Phebe) must agree to accept his (Silvius's) love, or have (i.e. since you do not want to have) a woman as your husband".

71 *sure together . . . weather* – "as firmly bound together as winter and stormy weather".

72 *Whiles . . . diminish* (125-7) – "While we sing a holy song in praise of marriage *(wedlock)*, satisfy yourselves by questioning one another, so that, knowing the reasons (for all these things), you will have less cause to wonder".

73 *Wedding* – "Marriage".

74 *Juno's crown* – "the best thing Juno has to offer". (Juno, the wife of Jupiter and so the queen of heaven, was regarded by the Romans as a goddess protecting women and blessing marriage.) Compare *crowned*, v.iii.30.

75 *bond of board and bed* – "bond joining man and woman day and night" (literally, "when they take their meals *(board)* and go to bed").

76 *welcome thou art . . . degree* – "I welcome you; just as much *(in no less degree)*, as if you were my own daughter".

HYMEN

Peace ho![65] I bar confusion:
'T is I must make conclusion
   Of these most strange events. 115
Here 's eight that must take hands
To join in Hymen's bands,[66]
   If truth holds true contents.[67]

[*To* ORLANDO *and* ROSALIND]
   You and you no cross[68] shall part:

[*To* OLIVER *and* CELIA]
   You and you are heart in heart:[69] 120

[*To* PHEBE]
   You to his love must accord,[70]
   Or have a woman to your lord:

[*To* TOUCHSTONE *and* AUDREY]
   You and you are sure together,[71]
   As the winter to foul weather.

[*To All*]
   Whiles[72] a wedlock hymn we sing, 125
   Feed yourselves with questioning,
   That reason may diminish,
   How thus we met, and these things finish.

Song

Wedding[73] is great Juno's crown:[74]
O blesséd bond[75] of board and bed! 130
'T is Hymen peoples every town;
High wedlock then be honouréd:
Honour, high honour, and renown,
To Hymen, god of every town!

DUKE SENIOR

O my dear niece, welcome thou art[76] to me! 135
Even daughter, welcome, in no less degree!

77 *eat my word . . . combine* – "take back my promise (to accept him in these circumstances – v.iv.15); and now you are my husband, your faithfulness to me binds *(doth combine)* my love *(fancy)* to you", i.e. she finds that she loves him after all and is not his merely because of her promise.

78 *Let . . . audience* – "Please listen to me". (Jaques de Boys, Orlando's second brother, has been mentioned only once – i.i.4 – and he appears here simply to report Duke Frederick's change of heart. Some critics have thought that Shakespeare originally planned to give him a larger part in the play.

79 *these tidings* – "this news".

80 *fair assembly* – "good company".

81 *great worth resorted* – "high rank were coming".

82 *Addressed . . . sword* (line 146) – "got ready a great army *(power)*, which he was leading himself, intending to capture his brother here (Duke Senior) and kill him".

83 *skirts* – "edge".

84 *old religious man*, i.e. an old man living alone, apart from the world, to study his religion. We are reminded of Rosalind's "old religious uncle" (iii.ii.298), but he was imaginary.

85 *question* – "serious discussion".

86 *converted . . . the world* – "changed in character and turned completely from the military action which he had started *(enterprise)*, as well as from life in the world (as distinct from life as a 'religious man')".

87 *his crown bequeathing* – "giving his power as a ruler".

88 *This to be . . . life* – "I pledge *(promise)* my life that this is the truth" (i.e. he is ready to be killed if it is not true).

89 *Thou offer'st fairly* – "You bring a good offering (i.e. present)".

90 *To one . . . withheld*, i.e. to Oliver, the family lands which Duke Frederick had kept back from him (iii.i.17).

91 *A land . . . dukedom* – "an entire country, a powerful *(potent)* state ruled by a duke". (By marrying Rosalind, Orlando has become Duke Senior's heir.)

92 *do those ends* – "finish the affairs" (i.e. complete the marriage ceremonies).

93 *well begun . . . begot:* The ceremonies had already begun happily in the forest, as was suitable *(well)* because they were the result of *(begot* by) forest life.

94 *every* – "every one".

95 *shrewd* – "hard".

96 *According . . . states* – "each according to his rank".

97 *new-fallen dignity* – "responsibility *(dignity)* which has just come to us".

PHEBE

[*To* SILVIUS] I will not eat my word,[77] now thou art mine;
Thy faith my fancy to thee doth combine.

Enter JAQUES DE BOYS

JAQUES DE BOYS

Let me have audience[78] for a word or two.
I am the second son of old Sir Rowland,   140
That brings these tidings[79] to this fair assembly.[80]
Duke Frederick, hearing how that every day
Men of great worth[81] resorted to this forest,
Addressed[82] a mighty power; which were on foot,
In his own conduct, purposely to take   145
His brother here and put him to the sword;
And to the skirts[83] of this wild wood he came;
Where, meeting with an old religious man,[84]
After some question[85] with him, was converted[86]
Both from his enterprise and from the world,   150
His crown bequeathing[87] to his banished brother,
And all their lands restored to them again
That were with him exiled. This to be true,[88]
I do engage my life.

DUKE SENIOR

Welcome, young man.
Thou offer'st fairly[89] to thy brother's wedding: 155
To one, his lands withheld;[90] and to the other,
A land itself at large,[91] a potent dukedom.
First, in this forest let us do those ends[92]
That here were well begun and well begot;[93]
And after, every[94] of this happy number,
That have endured shrewd[95] days and nights with us,
Shall share the good of our returnéd fortune,
According to the measure[96] of their states.
Meantime, forget this new-fallen[97] dignity,

98 *With measure . . . fall* – "with all possible joy, begin the dances" (playing on two meanings of *measure* – (i) container used for measuring; (ii) dance).

99 *by your patience* – "excuse me (for troubling you with my question)".

100 *The Duke . . . pompous court* – "Duke Frederick has adopted the life of a religious man and has lost all regard for the ceremonial *(pompous)* (life of the) court".

101 *To him will I* – "I shall go to him".

102 *these convertites* – "such people who have changed their way of living because of religion".

103 *is much matter* – "are many things".

104 *You to . . . bequeath* – "I leave you to (enjoy) your former honour". In parting from his friends, Jaques *bequeaths* (leaves as if in a will) their future lives to them.

105 *great allies* – "powerful friends". As the husband of Duke Senior's niece, and as the brother of the Duke's heir, the changed Oliver will have friends in high places.

106 *long*, i.e. to be enjoyed for a long lifetime.

107 *wrangling* – "arguing and quarrelling". Jaques does not believe that Touchstone and Audrey will live without quarrels for long. Their marriage, he suggests, is like a ship sailing on a long voyage with food supplies *(victualled*, line 180) for only two months: their loving patience will not last long.

108 *To see no pastime, I* – "I shall not stay to see any entertainment".

109 *what you would . . . know* – "I shall wait *(stay)* to be told what (service) you want me to do".

110 *rites* – "marriage ceremonies".

rustic revelry

238

And fall into our rustic revelry.   165
Play, music! And you brides and bridegrooms all,
With measure heaped[98] in joy, to the measures fall.

JAQUES

[*To* JAQUES DE BOYS] Sir, by your patience,[99] if I heard
   you rightly,
The Duke hath put on a religious life,
And thrown into neglect the pompous court.[100]   170

JAQUES DE BOYS

He hath.

JAQUES

To him will I:[101] out of these convertites[102]
There is much matter[103] to be heard and learned.
[*To* DUKE] You to your former honour[104] I bequeath;
Your patience and your virtue well deserve it.   175
[*To* ORLANDO] You to a love that your true faith doth merit:
[*To* OLIVER] You to your land, and love, and great allies;[105]
[*To* SILVIUS] You to a long[106] and well-deservéd bed;
[*To* TOUCHSTONE] And you to wrangling;[107] for thy loving
   voyage
Is but for two months victualled. So, to your pleasures: 180
I am for other than for dancing measures.

DUKE SENIOR

Stay, Jaques, stay.

JAQUES

To see no pastime,[108] I: what you would have,[109]
I 'll stay to know at your abandoned cave.   [*Exit*

DUKE SENIOR

Proceed, proceed: we will begin these rites,[110]   185
As we do trust they 'll end, in true delights.
                   [*A Dance; then Exeunt*

(Epilogue) Rosalind ends the play with a light, joking speech, mentioning that she is really a boy actor playing a girl's part, and hoping that *As You Like It* is "as the audience likes it".

1 *the lady the epilogue* – "the (actor who takes the part of the) leading lady speaking the epilogue".

2 *unhandsome* – "unsuitable".

3 *the lord the prologue* – "the actor in the chief male part giving the speech (that sometimes came) before the start of the play". (None of Shakespeare's comedies has a prologue. Six of the historical plays and tragedies have an opening speech, but not by the chief male character.)

4 *good wine . . . bush:* This common saying means that it is not necessary to draw attention to good things, since people find out about them for themselves. The reference is to the *bush* which used to hang outside an inn as a sign – like an advertisement.

5 *yet to good . . . bushes* – "in spite of that saying, such signs *are* used".

6 *a case am I in* – "an awkward situation I am in".

7 *nor cannot . . . behalf* – "and cannot cleverly win your approval for".

8 *furnished* – "dressed".

9 *conjure* – "appeal to" (with the idea of using "charm", as in the "conjuring" of magicians).

10 *charge you* – "demand of you" (said as if putting a magic charm to work on the audience).

11 *to like . . . please you* – Reminding the audience that the play is called *As You Like It*. Rosalind's "charge" is made jokingly, since what they like will of course please them!

12 *simpering* – "pleased smiling".

13 *If I were a woman:* Since Rosalind's part was played by a boy (see Introduction, p. xxvi).

14 *that liked me* – "that I liked".

15 *defied* – "scorned (as too bad)".

16 *for my kind offer,* i.e. Rosalind's kind offer to kiss them (if she were a woman).

17 *bid me farewell,* i.e. applaud.

good wine[4] *needs no bush*

Epilogue spoken by ROSALIND

It is not the fashion to see the lady[1] the epilogue; but it is no more
unhandsome[2] than to see the lord[3] the prologue. If it be true
that good wine[4] needs no bush, 't is true that a good play needs
no epilogue; yet to good wine they do use[5] good bushes, and
good plays prove the better by the help of good epilogues.   5
What a case[6] am I in then, that am neither a good epilogue, nor
cannot insinuate[7] with you in the behalf of a good play! I am
not furnished[8] like a beggar; therefore to beg will not become
me. My way is to conjure[9] you; and I 'll begin with the women.
I charge[10] you, O women, for the love you bear to men, to   10
like[11] as much of this play as please you; and I charge you, O
men, for the love you bear to women – as I perceive by your
simpering,[12] none of you hates them – that between you and
the women, the play may please. If I were a woman,[13] I would
kiss as many of you as had beards that pleased me, complexions   15
that liked[14] me, and breaths that I defied[15] not; and, I am sure,
as many as have good beards, or good faces, or sweet breaths,
will, for my kind offer,[16] when I make curtsy, bid me farewell.[17]

[Exit

GLOSSARY

This glossary explains all those words in the play which are used in Modern English as they were in Shakespeare's day, but are not among the 3,000 most-used words in the language.

The notes opposite the text explain words which are *not* used in Modern English. In these notes it has been necessary to use one or two words which are also outside the 3,000-word list; these are included in this glossary.

Explanations in the glossary are given entirely within the chosen list of words; only the meaning of the word as used in the text or notes is normally given.

v. = verb; n. = noun.

A

abhor, to hate.

abruptly, suddenly.

acorn, nut-like fruit of the oak tree.

adieu, (French) good-bye.

adoration, love amounting almost to worship.

alas, how sad (an expression of grief or regret).

amen, may it be so (said after a prayer).

ape, kind of monkey without a tail.

aside, (i) to the side of; (ii) (words) spoken by an actor and supposedly not heard by the other actors, e.g. when the actor is speaking secretly to himself or to the audience about the other actors on the stage.

assailant, attacker.

B

bachelor, unmarried man.

bankrupt, person who is known to be unable to pay his debts.

bark, outer covering or "skin" of a tree.

bask, to enjoy warmth.

bastinado, beating with a stick.

bell-wether, leading sheep of the flock (q.v.) with a bell on its neck (it is followed by the other sheep, so the sound of its bell leads the shepherd or his dog to the whole flock).

belly, stomach.

beloved, dearly loved.

bequeath, to leave (to a person) when one dies.

beseech, to beg (someone to do something).

beware, to take care (against some danger or harm).

bleak, cold and cheerless.

blush, to go red in the face with shame; (n.) *a blush*.

boar-spear, spear (q.v.) for hunting wild pigs *(boar)*.

boisterous, violent, rough.

bondage, slavery.

bramble, wild plant with sharp thorns growing as a bush or in hedges.

bride, woman on her wedding day; *bridegroom*, man on his wedding day.

brief, short, in few words; *briefly* or *in brief*, in few words.

brook, small stream.

C

caper, foolish trick (literally, a kind of leaping dance).

cast, to throw.

catechism, (i) a set of questions and answers on matters of Christian belief to be studied by young people; (ii) any set of questions and answers.

censure, blame.

challenge, to express a willingness to fight someone; *challenger*, one who declares he wants to fight the present winner.

charge, to order (someone to do something).

chase, to pursue, run after; (n.) *chase*.

chaste, pure in love; (n.) *chastity*.

chide (p.t. *chid*), to scold.

christen, to perform the ceremony giving a new-born child a name as a Christian.

civet, small cat-like wild animal from whose organs scent (also called *civet*) is obtained.

claw, sharp point on an animal's toe.

clown, (i) one who is employed to amuse others by his jokes; (ii) a simple countryman.

club, weapon in the form of a very thick short stick.

comedy, (light, amusing) stage play with a happy ending.

comment, to make a remark or remarks.

complexion, quality and colouring of the skin of the face.

consent, to agree (to something); (n.) agreement.

contemplation, serious thought; *contemplative*, thoughtful.

contents, that which is contained, e.g. what has been written in a letter.

counsel, (v.) to advise; (n.) advice; *counsellor*, one who advises, especially a ruler's advisers.

cur, dog of no value.

curtsy, a woman's polite greeting, by bending the knees and lowering the body.

D

damned, condemned to suffer punishment after death.

deny, to refuse to give something (I.ii.147, IV.iii.62).

depart, to go away; (n.) *departure*.

detained, made to stay.

devise, to plan.

discretion, the ability to decide what to do.

disdain, scorn.

disposition, habit of mind, character; *disposed*, in a state of mind.

dissuade, to persuade not to do something.

downright, plain; (adv.) plainly.

drunkard, man who regularly drinks to excess.

dug, part of a cow from which milk is drawn.

dunghill, a heap formed from the droppings of animals.

dyed, stained.

E

earthquake, violent shaking of the earth.

eke (out), to add to and make sufficient.

elegy, sad poem of regret.

emotion, strong feeling; *emotional*, concerned with the feelings rather than with reason.

emulation, rivalry.

endure, to bear something painful or unpleasant.

entreat, to beg to do (something); (n.) *entreaty*.

epilogue, speech at the end of a play.

errand, journey bearing a message.

ewe, female sheep.

executioner, man employed to put criminals to death.

exile, absence from one's own country.

extract, to draw out (juice from a plant, etc.).

F

farce, see Introduction, p. xxv.

fathom, measurement of depth (6 feet).

fell, animal's skin, fleece.

flock, (n.) sheep feeding and moving together; (v.) to go together in large numbers.

fly, (v.) to run away; (n.) *flight*.

foul, bad, harmful.

furnace, an arrangement for producing great heat to melt metals, etc.

G

gallows, wooden construction for hanging criminals.

gasp, short quick breath; *to the last gasp*, until death.

giddy, frequently changing one's mind; foolish.

gipsies, a wandering people, originally from India but believed (when they first appeared in England at the beginning of the sixteenth century) to be Egyptians, from which comes the name "gipsy".

glove, covering of leather (etc.) for the hand.

gout, a kind of illness bringing great pain to joints, especially that of the big toe.

grace, your, the correct way of addressing a duke.

graft, to put the stem of one plant in that of another so that a new kind of plant grows up.

grape, small soft fruit growing in bunches; grape juice makes wine.

Grecian, of the (ancient) Greeks; Greek.

H

hart, male deer.

hawk, to clear the throat noisily.

hawthorn, thorny bush with scented pale flowers.

heathen, non-Christian; ancient Greek or Roman.

highness, your, a respectful form of address to a prince or princess.

heel, back part of the foot.

henceforth, from this time on.

hind, female deer.

hoarse, having (suffering from) a rough voice.

holly, plant whose leaves remain green in winter.

huge, very large.

husk, dry outside covering of fruit, seeds, or grain.

I

idealism, believing that things can be as perfect as we think they ought to be; (adj.) *idealistic*.

inaccessible, very difficult to reach.

inconstant, always changing (especially in matters of love).

ingratitude, refusal to be kind when kindness is a duty owed to someone.

inseparable, that cannot be separated; (that were) never separated.

invisible, in a form that cannot be seen.

invocation, calling by the use of magic.

irony, (purposely) saying the opposite of what one really means (see Introduction, p. xxv); (adj.) *ironical*.

irrevocable, not to be withdrawn.

J

jolly, joyful.

jot, very small part.

K

knave, a wicked fellow; (n.) *knavery*.

knight, title of a nobleman lower in rank than a duke or lord but usually a landowner; the idea of a *knight* sometimes (e.g. III.ii.211) includes the wearing of armour and doing noble deeds as in stories of the Middle Ages.

L

lacklustre, dull.

lame, injured in the leg or foot and unable to walk.

lament, to feel or express grief for.

lass, girl (especially one with whom a man is in love).

libertine, person who lives to satisfy his own desires.

limb, arm or leg.

limp, to walk with difficulty and unevenly.

loath, very unwilling.

loathe, to dislike extremely.

lunacy, madness.

M

malice, wish to harm.

mar, to spoil.

martial, soldier-like.

marvel, to feel great surprise.

melancholy, (n.) sadness as a habit of mind; (adj.) sad in this way.

metaphor, see Introduction, p. xxiv.

misconstrue, to put the wrong meaning on.

miser, person who loves and stores up money, hating to spend it; (adj.) *miserly*.

monstrous, terribly wicked.

motley, the clothes, patched in many colours, of a court "fool".

murmur, to make a low continuous sound.

mustard, a hot-tasting yellow spice.

mutiny, to rebel.

N

nun, woman who for religious reasons has taken vows to live, with other women, a life of service; the form of a nun's service depends on the "order" of nuns of which she is a member.

O

oak, a kind of tree, which usually grows to a good height and breadth and has as its fruit the acorn; some oaks are of a very great age.

oath, (i) solemn promise made in the sight of God; (ii) bad language.

obscure, to cover up or hide.

ode, poem of praise.

ominous, giving a sign of approaching danger.

orator, public speaker.

orchard, piece of ground planted with fruit-trees.

overhear, to hear what is said privately to another person.

oyster, kind of shell-fish; pearls sometimes form within its shell.

P

pace, (i) way of moving (of a horse); (ii) step.

pancake, flat cake made of flour, eggs, and milk mixed and fried in a pan.

pasture, (i) field(s) of grass; (ii) grass as food for animals.

peasant, country man; worker on the land.

penury, extreme poverty.

people, (v.) to provide population for (v.iv.131).

perfumed, scented.

personify, *personification*. See Introduction, p. xxiv.

petticoat, woman's underskirt (at the time of the play women wore long petticoats showing below the outer skirt).

pilgrimage, journey made for religious reasons; *pilgrim*, person making such a journey.

profound, deeply learned.

promotion, being given a higher post or position.

prose, ordinary language, not controlled like verse.

provoke, to stir up, urge on.

punctuation, stops (, . ? etc.) to guide the reader.

purse, small bag for carrying money.

R

rail, to speak insultingly or scornfully.

ram, male sheep.

realism, seeing and describing things as they really are (the opposite of *idealism* q.v.); (adj.) *realistic*.

recompense (n. and v.) reward.

recount, to tell.

renown, fame.

requite, to reward.

resolute, determined.

revelry, rejoicing, merry-making.

ridiculous, laughably foolish.

romance, story of love and adventure, unlike the happenings of ordinary life; (adj.) *romantic*.

rustic, of the country and country people.

S

sanctify, to make holy; *sanctity*, holiness.

satchel, school bag (for carrying books).

savage, rough and fierce, like wild men or beasts.

scar, mark left by a wound.

scholar, man who is learned (usually one adding to his learning).

sensual, following the pleasures of the senses.

sermon, instruction given (in the form of a speech) in church.

servitude, being treated as a servant or slave.

shepherd, keeper of sheep; *shepherdess*, girl or woman employed to look after sheep.

shin, the leading edge of bone in a person's lower leg (easily hurt if knocked).

shun, to avoid meeting.

sigh, to take in a deep breath and then let it out in a way which can be heard (an indication of sadness); (n.) *a sigh*.

simile, see Introduction, p. xxiv.

sin, moral wickedness; *a sin*, an act of —.

snail, small creeping creature with soft body; it carries a curled shell on its back.

sob, to cry in sorrow.

solitary, lonely.

sound, to measure the depth of water.

sovereign, ruler.

spear, long wooden shaft with a metal point, used as a weapon.

spirits, state of mind.

spur, to make a horse run by pricking its side with a metal point attached to the rider's foot.

stag, male deer.

stammer, to speak nervously with pauses before certain sounds or with rapid repetition of the same sound before being able to continue.

stroke, to move the hand or fingers over.

sunder, to separate by force.

swift, quick, rapid.

swoon, to faint.

T

tale, story.

tar, thick black liquid which becomes hard when cooled (used to keep water out, cover holes, etc.); (v.) to apply tar.

tardy, late because of slowness.

taunt, to mock, trying to annoy.

tedious, wearying.

tenor, general meaning.

testament, a will or signed paper showing how one's possessions should be divided up after death.

thigh, upper part of the leg.

tradition, customary belief.

traitor, person who seeks to harm his country or its lawful ruler; *treason*, the act of a traitor.

transform, to change in shape.

turf, grass growing thickly on the ground.

tyrant, (i) unlawful ruler; (ii) cruel person without pity.

U

udder, part of female animal from which the young draw milk.

usurp, to seize power without right; *usurper*, a person who has done this.

V

valiant, brave.

venison, meat of the deer.

verge, edge.
vicar, priest serving a particular district.
videlicet, (Latin), that is to say.
vile, bad and hateful.
villain, wicked man; (adj.) *villainous*.
voluntary, of one's own choice.

W

wedlock, marriage.

weep, to cry, drop tears.
wheresoever, in whatever place.
whine, to complain in a high voice.
wholesome, healthy, health-giving.
wit, cleverness, good sense; *a wit*, a clever and amusing man.
woo, to try to win the love of someone; to persuade (I.iii.124); to seek (II.iii.50).
wrestle, to struggle with another man, each trying to throw the other down; (n.) *a wrestler*.